Autistic Spectrum Disorders

Spoken Language Difficulties: Practical Strategies and Activities for Teachers and Other Professionals by Lynn Stuart, Felicity Wright, Sue Grigor and Alison Howey
(ISBN 1-85346-855-X)

Accessing the Curriculum for Pupils with Autistic Spectrum Disorders: Using the TEACCH Programme to Help Inclusion by Gary Mesibov and Marie Howley
(ISBN 1-85346-795-2)

Autism in the Early Years: A Practical Guide by Val Cumine, Julie Leach and Gill Stevenson
(ISBN 1-85346-599-2)

Educational Provision for Children with Autism and Asperger Syndrome: Meeting their Needs by Glenys Jones
(ISBN 1-85346-669-7)

Autistic Spectrum Disorders Practical Strategies for Teachers and Other Professionals

Northumberland County Council Communication Support Service

 **David Fulton** Publishers

David Fulton Publishers Ltd
The Chiswick Centre, 414 Chiswick High Road, London W4 5TF
www.fultonpublishers.co.uk

First published in Great Britain in 2004 by David Fulton Publishers

David Fulton Publishers is a division of Granada Learning Limited, part of Granada plc.

British Library Cataloguing in Publication Data
A catalogue record for this book is available from the British Library.

ISBN 1-84312-155-7

Typeset by Pantek Arts Ltd, Maidstone, Kent
Printed and bound in Great Britain

Contents

Foreword

In recent years there have been some major developments for children and young people with autism that have had significant impacts on both the work and responsibilities of all staff employed in educational settings. The first is the generally accepted public and professional awareness that autism and autistic spectrum disorders (ASD) are much more common than previously recognised.[i] The second is the expectation that the majority of children will receive their education, as far as possible, within an inclusive education setting. For most this means within mainstream education.[ii,iii] Yet parents of children with ASD report that one of their key priorities is access to the most appropriate education for their children.[iv]

The National Autism Plan for Children[v] recommends that all community based staff working with children and young people should receive regular autism awareness training and that all schools should have whole-school awareness training as part of regular supported INSET provision at least once every three years. In addition many teaching and support staff will require specific training to educate and support affected individuals in their classrooms. Schools and other education settings will also need access to ASD education and intervention specialists able to advise and provide consultation about the specific social, communication and education needs of this group of young people.

There are an increasing number of publications and training opportunities for staff in educational settings to develop ASD specific assessment and teaching skills.[vi] However, for most schools and education authorities, there are enormous ongoing unmet needs for training and resources. This publication, written by members of a specialist peripatetic team, the Northumberland County Council Communication Support Service, provides a wealth of information about some of the areas of difficulty frequently encountered in schools. As the authors state in the Preface, not all children with ASD experience these types of difficulties, but this book covers 'the six main areas of school life affected by ASD'.

Autistic Spectrum Disorders: Practical Strategies for Teachers and Other Professionals provides a set of suggestions that will be of benefit as a training resource *and* of immediate practical support to school staff. The explanations for particular behaviours and difficulties provide everyday working examples that will make sense to staff. Suggested strategies and interventions can be lifted from the pages and put into place if appropriate.

This publication should be included in local training initiatives as well as a school-based resource that staff will want to use again and again. The format of the book is well organised for teachers and other school staff. First, staff choose an issue, read a possible explanation for the behaviour and, perhaps most importantly, read about specific sensible and practical advice that might help manage, anticipate or prevent the difficulty.

This excellent book will benefit pupils, teachers, support staff and all professionals working in schools. There is a good wide age range, from early school entry to high school curriculum concerns. The expertise of the authors shines out from the worked examples, the suggestions for IEP targets and the section on more general strategies.

Autistic spectrum disorders are unique in their pattern of deficits and areas of relative strengths. For each individual, the ability to progress will depend on many factors. Special needs are not static. They will vary with a child or young person's strengths, the impact of any other additional problems and diminish in situations where they are well met. Although this publication does not focus on the specific abilities of many individuals with ASD, the emphasis on school-based success through appropriate interventions will directly impact on each pupil's ability to achieve their own academic, social and communication potential.

Ann Le Couteur
Professor of Child and
   Adolescent Psychiatry
University of Newcastle
1–2 Claremont Terrace
Newcastle upon Tyne

September 2003

References

[i] Chakrabarti, S. and Fombonne, E. (2001) NAP-C, p. 112

[ii] Jordan, R. and Jones, G. (1999) NAP-C, p. 114

[iii] DfES (2001) NAP-C, p. 117

[iv] English, A. and Essex, J. (2001) NAP-C, p. 113

[v] Le Couteur, A., Baird, G. and NIASA (2003)

[vi] *ASD Good Practice Guidance* (2001) www.dfes.gov.uk/sen

Notes on contributors

The contributors are all members of the Northumberland County Council Communication Support Service peripatetic team.

Jennie Beckwith trained and worked as a teacher before gaining a BSc in Speech and Language Sciences and qualifying as a speech and language therapist.

Amanda Cuthbertson has worked as a speech and language therapist in mainstream, special schools and a language unit. She is also a qualified teacher.

Rosamund Davison is a teacher with experience in a wide range of settings. She has DAES in Child Language and Language Disability and was head of a language unit based in a special school.

Sue Grigor is Head of the Communication Support Service. She is a teacher, has an MEd in Child Language and Language Disability and is currently completing a PhD in Speech Sciences. She is a co-author of *Spoken Language Difficulties: Practical Strategies and Activities for Teachers and Other Professionals* (David Fulton Publishers 2002).

Alison Howey is a teacher with experience in a wide range of settings in three different countries. She has an MEd in Child Language and Disability. She is also a qualified teacher of children with hearing impairments and is a co-author of *Spoken Language Difficulties*.

Lynn Stuart is the principal author of this book and of *Spoken Language Difficulties*. She is also the author of many educational books including *Cloze Plus* (Hodder & Stoughton) under the name of Lynn Hutchinson, and has contributed to various journals and publications. She is a teacher with a DAES in Child Language and Language Disability.

Felicity Wright is the Deputy Head of the Communication Support Service. She gained a BSc in Speech Sciences and worked as a speech and language therapist before taking a PGCE and qualifying as a teacher. She is also a co-author of *Spoken Language Difficulties*.

Preface

Increasing numbers of children are recognised as experiencing an autistic spectrum disorder, and educational provision for most of these children is found within a mainstream school. Autistic spectrum disorders (ASDs) are also sometimes referred to as pervasive development disorders because they pervade so many areas of life and are intrinsic to that individual's development.

We have identified six main areas in which children with ASD have the most difficulty in our schools: behaviour, learning and thinking, conversation, sensory and motor experiences, language and communication, and social skills. This book is designed to help concerned adults in school identify the area of difficulty, understand the reason for the particular behaviour, and give practical advice to change, moderate or manage these difficulties within mainstream schools.

Not all children with ASD experience all these difficulties in all these areas. However, because ASD is quite frequently accompanied by other conditions such as attention deficit hyperactivity disorder (ADHD), dyspraxia and dyslexia, some children have considerable difficulties in most of these areas.

The areas of difficulty diagram (Fig. 1.1, p. 1) shows the six main areas of school life affected by ASD. The map can be photocopied and used as a checklist by highlighting areas of most concern. The index of areas of difficulty (pp. 121–2) refers to the relevant section of the book where suggestions and ideas helpful to the specific areas of concern can be found. Suggested individual education plan (IEP) targets are also included at the end of each section.

For the sake of convenience the child is referred to as 'he' throughout this book and the teacher as 'she'.

Acknowledgements

We would like to acknowledge the school staff who have highlighted the needs of pupils with ASD in their schools and responded with enthusiasm to the suggestions and support provided by the authors. The most useful strategies, developed with pupils and staff, are described in this book.

Thanks also go to specialists in health and education working in Northumberland, and further afield, who have contributed, through personal contact, joint working, courses, and books, to the knowledge and professional development of the peripatetic teachers working for the Northumberland County Council Communication Support Service.

Thanks also go to Donna Williams for permission to quote from her book *Nobody Nowhere – The Remarkable Autobiography of an Autistic Girl*, and to Luke Jackson for permission to quote from his book *Freaks, Geeks and Asperger Syndrome – A User Guide to Adolescence*, both published by Jessica Kingsley Publishers, and to Clare Sainsbury for permission to quote from her book *Martian in the Playground – Understanding the Schoolchild with Asperger's Syndrome*, published by Lucky Duck Publishing Ltd.

Areas of difficulty

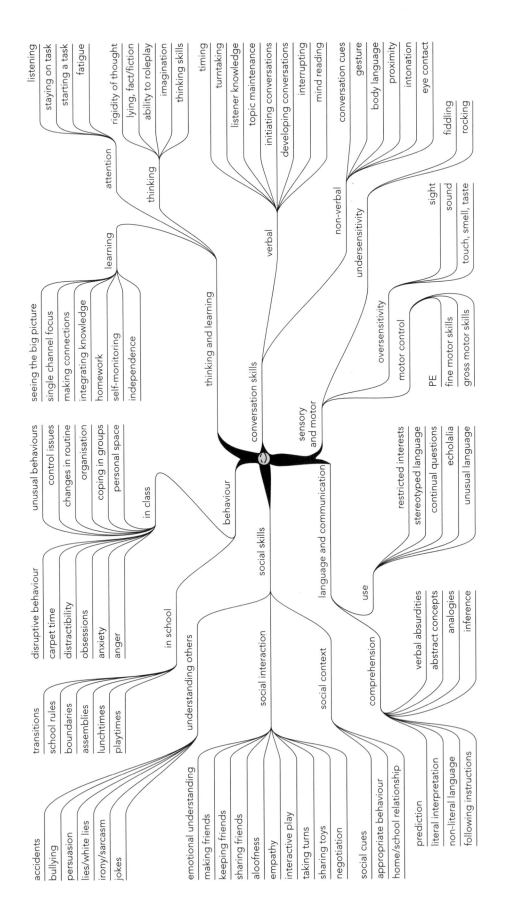

Figure 1.1 Mindmap of areas of difficulty: the child with ASD in school

Chapter 1: Behaviour

School 1

Playtimes

Social and communication skills are developed mainly during play periods but children with ASD may miss out because many of them find playtimes difficult. They may not know where they can and can't go, with whom, when, what and how they can play. They find social interaction difficult and can't just 'let off steam' like other children.

The level of adult supervision and structure is not usually the same as that found in class and in these conditions their behaviour can deteriorate. There may be sensory factors such as the noise and movement of other children which affect the child. The weather, especially wind, may disturb him.

Challenging behaviour from the child usually means that he is anxious, frustrated and/or fearful.

Strategies

- Organise clearly marked boundaries and make sure all the children know which areas are out of bounds and under what conditions, for example, when it has been raining, when the library van visits, etc. Picture symbols or digital photographs may help.

- Ensure that the playground rules are clear – particularly bullying procedures and lining up – and imposed consistently.

- An adult could teach and lead some children's games to include the child with ASD.

- Consider using peer group support at playtimes so that responsibility is shared by the class for including the child, perhaps setting them a task or game. Older children may take it in turns to include the child in their social group (see Playtime strategies in Section 2).

- Allocate an area of the playground for those children who wish to sit and be quiet.

- Set aside another area in the playground where the child will be safe to run about, flap or talk to himself if he feels the need.

- Arrange for a 'safe base' within school. This should be a staffed, peaceful and secure area to which a child can withdraw if he cannot cope with the stress of playtimes.

- Set up clubs so that the child can indulge in a recreational activity.

- Current IEP targets relevant to playtime behaviour should be available to all playtime duty staff.

- If the child finds communication difficult, ensure that procedures are in place to alert an adult to the fact that he needs help such as a card kept in his pocket which he can show to the supervisor.

- A pupil profile of the child should be available so that new and temporary members of staff know for whom to look. This could contain a photo and brief description of what the child can/can't do, how situations should be handled and what specific strategies may be in use.

- Keep a notebook handy so that any improved or deteriorating behaviour can be noted in order to find triggers to the change in behaviour or for pattern recognition.

School 2

Lunchtimes

A dining hall can be an extremely noisy place – the sounds of clattering plates, chinking of cutlery, scraping of chairs and conversation bounce off hard surfaces. This can be physically painful for some acutely sensitive ASD children. Others cannot screen out the noise, which remains constantly in the background causing genuine distress. These children may need to eat their lunch in another, quieter area, at least until some tolerance has been acquired.

A separate room in which to eat packed lunches may be a better option, or in extreme cases, the child may need to have his lunch apart from the others, perhaps in his 'safe base' or at a slightly different time.

Many children with ASD are rigid in their eating habits, sticking to a restricted range of foods. Sometimes they will eat a food at school that they will violently reject at home and vice versa. Some children need more time to chew and swallow. In all cases, try to keep the child calm to ensure that lunchtime is as stress-free and enjoyable as possible.

Make sure the child knows the routines – hand-washing, queuing, where to keep lunch, where to eat it, what to do with waste, dirty plates/lunchbox, glasses etc. Some children will benefit from a visual timetable so that they can see the overall structure and find their way through it.

Strategies

- Prepare the young child by visiting the dining hall when it is empty and again when everything is set up just before the children come in. Show him where different things are and what he will do.
- Label the areas he needs to know (pictures or photos may be more helpful).
- Create a visual schedule if necessary and use it to teach him routines he needs to know. This can either be displayed or provided on a card kept in his pocket.
- Appoint a lunchtime supervisor to whom he can turn for help. There should be a prearranged signal such as a card he can show if he is unable to communicate his difficulty and is in need of assistance.
- Use one other child, or a small group, to help him cope with the routines.
- Imagine yourself in his place and try to anticipate any specific difficulties he is likely to experience. Be flexible about timing and physical arrangements.
- Liaise with parents – they are an invaluable source of information regarding eating patterns and preferences, and may be able to help avert difficulties in school.
- Make sure the relevant supervisors are aware of any IEP target related to the child's behaviour at lunchtimes so they can implement agreed strategies and monitor achievement.
- Prepare the child for any changes in routine.
- If there are any issues relating to the child not eating enough it may be helpful to create a picture sequence for him to follow. A packed lunch is best in this respect to allow time to prepare pictures/photos of the contents of his lunchbox.

School 3

Assemblies

Taking part in an assembly in a school hall can be very difficult for many children with ASD because of the different acoustics and the noise, movement and proximity of other children. Visual and other distractions make it difficult for them to focus on the proceedings.

In order to feel secure, some children with ASD try to control the environment by indulging in behaviour such as rocking and making noises. Other children put a sensory barrier between themselves and the world beyond by blinking, flapping or making sounds. With other children in such close proximity, children with ASD may repeatedly touch those near to them, behaviour that might go unnoticed by a teacher too far away to be able to see and intervene.

Children with ASD may not know where they belong because they are in a different place each time. They may not understand what is expected of a pupil in assembly or find it difficult to comply when normal classroom structures are not in place. Assemblies are different and unpredictable. There may be visiting speakers, class assemblies, performances, music and clapping. There may or may not be contributions from the children – this is bewildering and may result in inappropriate behaviour.

In the event of a difficulty with a child's behaviour in assembly, it should be regarded as inappropriate rather than naughty, a probable result of situational stress. Try to identify possible triggers within the environment and determine if they can be removed or the situation modified. The ultimate aim is for the child to be included like any other pupil; in order to achieve this, a gradual, step-by-step approach may be required.

Other pupils may need to be aware of the child's social difficulties (perhaps through PSHE for older pupils) and encouraged to respond in the way requested by the teacher, for example by ignoring certain behaviours.

Strategies

- Take the child into the hall for a smaller class assembly, rather than a year or whole-school assembly, until he becomes more comfortable with the surroundings.
- Arrange for the child to sit or stand in a particular place, close to the teacher, using marker tape or a carpet square if necessary.
- Make sure the child is near good role models and sympathetic children.
- If there are particular parts of the assembly the child finds especially upsetting plan to take him out **before** that point is reached (not as a reward for his difficult behaviour).
- Try bringing the child into assembly for the last couple of minutes and then slowly extend the time.
- Prepare the child for the assembly, particularly for any changes.
- Try to find more socially acceptable alternatives for his behaviour, such as giving him something to hold which is silent, like a stress-squeezer.
- Include a target on his IEP for specific behaviour in assemblies. Make sure he knows the target and is willing to change his behaviour. Decide and implement strategies to promote the desired change such as a reward system, a specially written social story and informing parents via the home/school book (see Section 2).

School 4

Boundaries

Children with ASD may not be aware of boundaries. They may have difficulty working things out for themselves so will need to be taught. They should be told about physical boundaries in school such as which toilets and rooms not to go into, which rooms can be entered after knocking and hearing an answer, and which can and cannot be entered with and without adult permission.

These children will not necessarily learn by example, i.e. seeing others obey the rules or practising safety strategies such as walking on the left in the corridor to avoid bumping into other people.

Children with ASD are often unaware of social boundaries. They may be over-familiar with strangers, ask adults inappropriate questions such as their age, comment on others' appearances, repeat catchphrases and generally irritate and upset others by their endless comments. These examples also reveal their lack of empathy and social awareness, and their inability to read subtle non-verbal cues that are vital to facilitate communication. This is all part of the difficulty with mind reading (see Ch. 2, Mind reading).

Strategies

- Be very explicit when telling a child where he can and can't go.
- Use pictures/photos of restricted areas and make sure the child knows and understands them.
- Be clear about changes in the boundary rules such as when it is his turn to play in the sand and when he must not play. Use symbols or pictures as reinforcement.
- Explain what is inappropriate about specific behaviours, even if he does not fully understand the reasons. Try to suggest something else he can do instead.
- Reward efforts to change through whatever gives him greater motivation.
- If there is a particular problem over boundaries include a target in his IEP. Make sure he knows the target and is willing to change his behaviour. Decide and implement strategies to promote the desired change such as a reward system, a specially written social story and informing parents via the home/school book (see Section 2).

School 5

School rules

As stated above, a child with ASD cannot easily work out the rules from his observations of the behaviour of other children. He finds it hard to read non-verbal cues/clues and to see the bigger picture, such as understanding that the school rules exist to make school a happy and safe place to be.

He may not be able to work out the meaning of rules such as 'be kind to others' as this would involve imagining himself in someone else's shoes, a mind-reading skill which children with ASD develop very slowly. He may have to be told categorically not to deliberately hurt others. Children with these difficulties often respond better to visual information or they may respond to written rules – it may be helpful to display them for reference.

Some rules are implicit and may not have been consciously taught, such as how to sit and listen at carpet time. These should be taught by demonstration and put on cards to be kept on desks or displayed on the wall.

A child with ASD, with his own innate sense of right and wrong, may try to impose rules on others. He will have difficulty in interpreting when and why a rule can be relaxed, for example, in a medical emergency. Some children 'tell tales' because they are unaware of social context and consequences – they simply see another child doing something wrong and seek to correct or punish the wrongdoer.

Strategies

- Make rules explicit, realistic and unambiguous. Display and refer to them regularly.
- Emphasise that the rules apply to the whole class/school, not just to the child.
- Be consistent in their application.
- Make sure any sanctions for breaking them are fair (which does not necessarily mean they should be the same for all children).

School 6

Transitions

For many children, changing from Key Stage 2 to 3 also involves changing schools. Although the transition from Key Stage 3 to 4 usually takes place within the same school, it still involves considerable organisational changes as well as more demanding academic requirements. In addition, the change from Key Stage 2 to 3 usually heralds the end of class-based learning – pupils have to start moving around the building(s) to different specialist areas. This can be very difficult for children with ASD who do not cope well with changes and rely heavily on routines – this in turn will create problems for teachers meeting these pupils for the first time.

In every case involving major changes, thorough preparation is the best way to ease the transition.

Strategies

- If the transition involves moving school, the child with ASD may benefit from more than one visit – perhaps on his own the first time and later with his cohort. It may be helpful if he could be accompanied by a member of staff who knows him well, such as a learning support assistant (LSA). This adult can be made aware of those features of the new school which may cause distress and for which preparation must be made.
- A map of the school showing different routes is useful. Walk the child through the building(s), perhaps at a quiet time or after school.
- If the old and new schools are in close proximity, perhaps the LSA could spend the first week with the child in the new school, passing on her skills and knowledge to the new LSA.
- If possible the pupil should meet his new LSA, mentor, ASD co-ordinator and form tutor prior to his first day at the new school – not necessarily all at once! Showing the child a photo of relevant staff may be helpful as preparation.
- Training for special educational needs co-ordinators (SENCOs), form tutors, and LSAs who will be working with the children more closely may be required as well as training on the implications of admitting pupils with ASD.
- One designated teacher within each school should be appointed as the ASD co-ordinator responsible for the ASD pupils and liaison with other staff and parents (see Section 2, The older pupil – a whole-school approach).
- Each child should have a mentor to whom he can turn, perhaps at specified times, when he is in need of help and support.
- Create a pupil profile for the receiving staff and school to include an up-to-date photo, a pen picture describing the pupil's personality, strengths and weaknesses in subject areas and school life, trigger points, useful management strategies and current IEPs.
- Ensure all subject teachers who are likely to encounter the child have a copy of this pupil profile.
- Create a 'safe base' where children can be withdrawn from lessons by teachers and support assistants depending on the level of need. This should be a calm, low-distraction room that will help to promote 'on task' behaviour.
- Use a staffed 'safe base' for playtimes and lunchtimes for those pupils who may need to retreat if they find the mainstream environment too stressful.
- Photograph the interior of every room the child is likely to use. Include symbols for the specific activities that take place in each room and a photograph of the teacher (which can be updated as staff change).

Class 1

Anxiety

Adults with ASD describe high levels of anxiety arising from their bewilderment at not knowing what is expected of them in different social situations, not understanding the 'rules' of interaction and how they are applied in different contexts, fear of the reactions of others and their emotions, and fear of change (see Section 3).

Many children with ASD also experience distressing levels of anxiety in school. Each child has his own way of displaying and coping with anxiety.

These behaviours generally indicate anxiety:

- echolalia (repeating the last few words of what has been said to him);
- inappropriate volume (too loud, too soft);
- repetitive questions;
- inappropriate laughter;
- destructive behaviour.

These behaviours demonstrate that the child is trying to cope with anxiety by:

- obsessive interests and/or repetitive play to promote predictability and security;
- blinking, turning lights and switches on and off to slow things down;
- repeating words so that the meaning is lost and just the sound patterns remain;
- spinning, whirling objects and focusing on bright and sparkly objects as a means of cutting themselves off from others;
- imposing their own agenda to maintain control – it is difficult for them to abide by the rules, routine and rituals of others.

An anxious child is not going to make the most of being in school so it is in everyone's interests to try to reduce anxiety levels.

Strategies

- Create a safe, supervised area where the child can go if he is having problems coping in class or at playtimes/lunchtimes.
- Ensure clear, structured, unambiguous routines are in place to help to reduce anxiety. Use visual schedules (see Section 2).
- Gradually build in a choice of activities and small alterations to the daily routine using the visual schedule.
- Avoid sudden changes – provide clear warnings of when one activity is to end and another will start.
- Use the visual schedule to prepare for changes, e.g. what happens when he is late for school because of a hospital appointment.
- Reduce stimuli which might contribute to a sensory overload such as noise, movement, lights, colours and stimulating art displays.
- Do not expect the child to be able to multitask. Children with ASD often have difficulty receiving information via more than one channel at a time, or behaving in a way that involves more than one skill at a time (e.g. talk and show).
- Do not be too direct in approach (which many children find threatening) – stand beside the child rather than in front of his face to talk to him.

Class 2

Anger

Children with ASD can sometimes respond angrily to a stimulus in a way that seems disproportionate because:

- the child is angered by situations and events others do not see as particularly frustrating or 'anger-making' and therefore have not predicted;
- the child is not conscious of the build-up of tension until it is too late;
- the child cannot make an alternative appropriate response because he is not aware of the moment of choice;
- the child cannot 'measure' his response in relation to the strength and nature of the stimuli.

Situations that result in eruptions of anger are best tackled by:

- modifying the environment and any external factors that may create stress and anger;
- helping the child to recognise his trigger points and his changed physical state, and plan his response.

Strategies

- Note when anger occurs and identify warning signs.
- If possible, avoid those situations likely to produce an angry response.
- Avoid confrontation and keep your voice calm. Do not allow it to carry overtones of emotion – keep it neutral and impersonal.
- Try distracting the child to a preferred activity he usually finds enjoyable.
- Always make it clear what you **want** the child to do rather than just what you **don't** want him to do.
- Agree on a prompt card or signal which can be used by the adult to direct the child to use alternative behaviour – such as go to a certain place and sit down, get a drink of water or whatever has been agreed – when an angry response is building up. Practise the strategy in role play beforehand.
- When a particular strategy works, make sure all other staff likely to be involved with the child are aware of it. It should be applied consistently and without variation.
- Help the child to accept that he may be angry because he has misunderstood something and may be wrong.

Section 4 (Resources) suggests books and schemes to help the child recognise and cope with his own angry feelings. They involve helping the child accept that:

- everyone feels anger at some time or other – it is OK to feel angry but not to hurt and upset others;
- there are levels of anger which give rise to different feelings;
- there are good and bad ways of expressing anger;
- expressing anger in a bad way has negative effects.

These books also include activities to help the child understand his angry feelings and to help staff to determine the appropriate responses before an incident occurs.

Class 3

Disruptive behaviour

Disruptive behaviour affects the smooth running of the class and perhaps also other children's experience and access to the curriculum. The child with ASD may call out and distract other children, sometimes by touching them. He may be physically restless and run away.

Some disruptive behaviour arises out of profound dislike of some experience, or even phobia, which can cause the child severe distress. While his response may seem irrational, it is valid to him and should be respected as such. Only very small and gradual exposures to certain situations are acceptable in order to build tolerance – if possible with the permission and co-operation of the child – supported by a strategy such as a social story and/or a visual schedule (see Section 2).

The child with ASD may be disruptive because of an angry reaction caused by frustration (see Anger (above) for strategies to help).

Strategies

- Do not raise your voice or become angry – maintain a neutral and unemotional tone.
- If possible make physical changes to the classroom to prevent injury or escape.
- If practical and appropriate, have an area or room with soft cushions and no furniture or equipment which can cause injury.
- If necessary, ensure the child is not within the reach of other children if this is a problem, especially in assemblies, circle time, carpet time etc. when all the children would be sitting close together. He may need a special space, chair or carpet tile near the teacher, perhaps with something comforting to hold.
- Note when, where and with whom disruptive incidents occur so that triggers can be found and situations prevented when possible.
- Try to understand why these incidents happen through your knowledge of the child.
- Endeavour to find out how the child perceives the situation so you can talk about it and shift his perceptions, explaining the effect of his behaviour on others.
- Use a social story to support change (see Section 2).
- With the child, set a realistic target on his IEP with clear strategies as to how this is to be achieved and the criteria for success.

Class 4

Obsessions

Children with ASD usually have all-absorbing narrow interests which persist over time to the exclusion of all other topics. When young, these interests may centre around Thomas the Tank Engine and dinosaurs, but as they grow older these earlier interests are superseded by subjects which require an almost encyclopaedic detailed knowledge about one or a few narrow areas of interest such as timetables. They do not usually involve piecing information together in a novel and creative way, and do not generally demand knowledge, experience or an attraction for human interactions involving empathy and imagination – soap operas and dramas high in emotional content are of little interest to children with ASD. School interests are unlikely to include arts subjects which involve subjective responses – maths, science and IT are subjects generally preferred.

A child with ASD will often talk about his interests in an obsessive way and try to impose his topic of conversation. He is often only interested in others insofar as they share his interests, and cannot understand that others do not necessarily share a passion for these same hobbies. As he cannot read non-verbal cues, he is frequently unaware when others have lost interest.

Repetitive play and obsessive interests do undoubtedly help to reduce stress in children with ASD but they may be a substitute for real conversations and imaginative play which the child finds difficult – too much time spent on the preferred subject will reduce the time available for practising other sorts of interaction.

Strategies

- Allocate specific times or places when the child's favoured topic of conversation can be discussed. Deflect discussion at other times, gently but firmly returning the child to the activity in hand.
- Give the child 'talk tickets' as a reward for successfully completing a teacher-directed task which he can exchange for time to talk on his chosen topic.
- If possible, use the favourite topic to practise conversational skills, perhaps including one or two other children.
- Try to extend the favourite topic and relate it to other similar topics – even to the current teaching topic where possible.

Class 5

Unusual behaviours

Many younger children with ASD flap their hands when excited. It is only when they become older that this becomes of concern as it makes them conspicuous and may attract unwelcome comments from others who do not understand. Sometimes this and other unusual behaviours can be discussed and explained through PSHE and in special assemblies to help increase other children's understanding, tolerance and acceptance.

Other ASD children may blink their eyes, grimace, rock, laugh inappropriately, repeat phrases endlessly, sniff and make noises among other things. Do not prevent or stop the activity but accept it as an expression of pleasure or a source of some comfort to the child by relieving stress. If there is a genuine need to change or moderate the behaviour, it is necessary to find an alternative acceptable to the child. As in all attempts to change behaviour – particularly with an older child – the child should be involved, understanding if not sharing the need for change and accepting the adoption of more socially acceptable behaviour.

Strategies

- Involve the child in identifying the behaviour to be changed. Decide exactly what can be done, where and for how long, for example, agree that he will not make a certain noise for say ten minutes in a specified lesson. This can be extended to not making noises in class at all, however, it may be acceptable for him to make these noises in the playground. The child can be involved in monitoring how successful he is on a lesson-by-lesson basis, perhaps through the use of a record card or star chart completed at the end of each lesson. He could report to his teacher/mentor at the end of each day for positive reinforcement.
- Set this as a target in his IEP.
- Write a specific social story for each circumstance (see Section 2).

Class 6

Distractibility

Many children with ASD are distractible, particularly when young. Some researchers have described it as like being a baby when all stimuli are equally valid – the temperature of the room, the weight and touch of clothes on the skin, the movement of air, sounds, movements, colours, internal thoughts, feelings and images. As we mature we learn to focus on what is important to us and do not pay attention to stimuli of low priority.

It is thought that ASD children do not have the same priorities because they do not get the same pleasure from the same activities as the majority of children without ASD (sometimes called neuro-typicals or NTs). They do not all develop the ability to screen out what is unimportant, perhaps because their ideas of relevance and interest are different from others and perhaps because they do not have the ability to prioritise items of importance from the vast sensory input we are all assaulted by every day. Perhaps even when they can select what requires their attention they cannot maintain that decision for long because of the competition from other stimuli. Many children with ASD have altered sensory perceptions (see Ch. 4 on sensory and motor skills).

Children with distractibility difficulties will only learn slowly how to stay on task and ignore what is not relevant. They cannot easily change, therefore changes need to be made to their environment in order to provide them with optimum conditions to support their efforts.

Strategies

- Use a visual schedule (see Section 2) so the child knows what he should be doing and where at all times.
- Gain his attention by saying his name before giving verbal instructions.
- Make sure work areas are known or delineated in class so boundaries are clear.
- The child should be allowed to carry a prompt card with a picture (or words) of the activity he should be doing in order to remind himself to return to task.
- He may need a prompt card to show whether he should be talking or listening, and who will be deciding on the task, i.e. teacher or child.
- Set up a work station where the child can be instructed separately or can work on his own without distraction (see Section 2).
- Keep the classroom as distraction-free as possible and ensure that the child is not in close proximity to noisy heaters, corridors and low windows. Christmas decorations and dangling displays of art work which move in the breeze can be difficult for some children.
- Set up a 'focus room' or area, in neutral colours, containing minimum distractions where children who need to can go and work.

Class 7

Carpet time

Carpet time can prove exceptionally difficult for children with ASD. They may easily lose concentration, they may find the proximity of other children uncomfortable or want to touch them, especially their hair.

Some children need to be in exactly the same space every time and cannot tolerate change. If the children are in a circle, the child may have to be pointed in the right direction and not facing outwards – unless he can only pay attention to what he hears if he is not distracted by what he sees. If this is the case, let him look away for instruction, turning away if necessary. However, as most people with ASD are visual learners, the children need to learn where to look for information. Do not talk and show at the same time but allow a little time between instructions and information and the visual stimulus or reinforcement, for the child to take it in.

Many children find it hard to follow conversations between two or more people because they do not know where to look and their eye contact is poor.

Sometimes the child may come out with a badly timed and apparently irrelevant response triggered by something he has heard; this is a classic example of the difficulties these children experience with understanding what is appropriate.

Strategies

- Make sure all the children understand expected carpet time behaviour. The rules should be written, displayed and referred to as 'rules'. They can be specially adapted to suit the particular class, such as 'Yellow Class Carpet Time Rules', e.g.

    look at the teacher
    listen carefully
    keep quiet
    sit still

- Use the social filing cabinet (see Section 2) to illustrate undesirable behaviour.

- Seat the child in his special place (chair, carpet tile) between good role models or beside an adult if he needs reminders to focus and listen.

- Decide how long the carpet session will last and use a poster or clock to inform the child of how much longer he has to sit.

- Avoid long periods of sitting as this encourages restlessness or passivity. Try to break up periods of instruction with other activities, or with 'fidget time' – a minute or two to wriggle, stretch or move about.

- Preface comments and instructions with the child's name to maintain his attention.

- Give the child something to hold if he has difficulty keeping his hands still. Rehearse appropriate behaviours for when he wants to say something while the teacher is talking, such as putting up his hand. Include this as an IEP target and make explicit exactly what he should do in a social story (see Section 2).

- Introduce a reward scheme for good carpet time behaviour.

Class 8

Following own agenda

A frequent comment made about children with ASD is that, for many, all interactions are on their own terms and that the children operate according to their 'own agendas'.

This need to control situations arises out of fear of the unpredictable and unknown. Adult autistics describe how 'rules' learned in one situation are not transferred to other situations because the situations are never exactly the same. As a consequence they are unprepared for many situations and are in a continual state of new learning. This can be exhausting and without reward. They may try to cope by imposing a behaviour learned in one situation to another whether or not it is appropriate. A person with ASD needs to be able to live by his own, not others' rules, rituals and routines, starting and finishing according to his needs. If he controls the situation by deciding what he will do or talk about, when, with whom and for how long, then he can avoid discomfort and distress.

A child may maintain control through repetition, obsessions, lining things up and putting them in order, and always doing things a certain way. Some children need to have their pencil case in a certain place, or pencils and pens arranged in certain positions. Some children want their work to be perfect so are continually rubbing out, wasting learning time and losing concentration.

Sometimes the child does something to deliberately shock, to prove he can manipulate the reactions of others and that he is in control.

Strategies

- Be prepared to negotiate with regard to what must be done or talked about; for example, the child agrees to do what he is asked by the teacher until 3.05pm when he can choose another activity or talk about what he likes until it is time to go home.
- See if other anxieties can be removed or reduced so that the child does not have to maintain the same degree of control in order to cope.
- Try to extend the child's agenda by introducing new challenges gradually as a means to increase tolerance and flexibility.

Class 9

Changes in routines

As previously stated, children with ASD like everything to be predictable and therefore are very resistant to changes in routine. They have a strong desire for 'sameness' because it is expected and reassuring, and may even find changing activities difficult.

The child with ASD needs careful preparation for change – not necessarily too far ahead but long enough for him to get used to the idea that the change is going to happen. He needs to know what will take place instead of the usual arrangements and that someone will be available should he require help. He needs to rehearse – either physically or in his head – the sequence of the day's events. Visual support will also be necessary to help him establish his position in the order of change.

Obviously some changes occur without notice. A bus taking the children swimming may break down, resulting in the children having to travel on a double-decker bus rather than a single decker. It can be useful to think about other conceivable alterations in routine, how they can be managed and discuss them with the child.

Strategies

- Use the visual schedule or transition planners to prepare for known events such as changes of teacher, classroom or assembly time, and routines such as arriving late at school because of a hospital appointment etc. (see Section 2).

- Prepare the child at the beginning of each day and check that he knows about any changes.

- Always prepare the child for new experiences such as starting circle time; try to avoid unannounced changes.

- Give a warning that a change of activity is going to happen to prepare the child who has difficulty with transitions. It may help to provide continuity if he takes a toy with him from one activity to another.

- When the child has coped successfully with a change which previously he would have found difficult, celebrate this with him in a way he finds meaningful.

Class 10

Organisation

Another characteristic typical of many children with ASD is difficulty organising themselves and their belongings. They may have problems with time and space, mislay books and equipment, forget to do/hand in homework and leave their PE kits at home.

Strategies

- Colour code the child's books and equipment so it is easily identifiable.
- Ensure there is enough labelled storage space in the classroom for the child's needs in school.
- Keep what he needs to bring to school, or carry round, to a minimum.
- Develop and maintain good links with home to help the child. Send home an equipment list.
- In class, a task sheet can be used to tick off work as it is completed (see Section 2, Organisation strategies).
- Use a portable visual schedule or transition planner so the child knows where he should be and what he should be doing at any one time (see Section 2).
- Use visual techniques to help the sequencing of tasks and activities such as flowcharts and mindmaps.
- Ask the child to report at specified intervals for checking – three sums, ten minutes etc.
- Give plenty of notice before the end of the lesson.
- Allow extra time for packing up equipment etc.
- Be clear about what is required, when it is finished and what to do then.
- Allow plenty of time for information to be processed and check understanding.
- If it is acceptable to the child, consider using a buddy to help check that he has everything he needs to take home (see Section 2).
- Be consistent in classroom expectations, particularly in respect of the organisation of time and space. For example:

  Work from left to right at all times including tabletop activities.
  Sit next to the child when demonstrating tasks, not opposite.
  Link time concepts in a left to right framework, useful later for timetables, flowcharts etc.
  Make a visual record of events, e.g. record what the child sees, hears and does as they occur, left to right.
  Use advent calendars, diaries etc. to reinforce the visual representation of time.
  Talk about **now**, what has **already happened** and what is **going to happen**.
  Establish concepts of **first, next, last** in space and time, as in:
  Who is **first** in line? What did I do **first**? Which letter comes **next**?
  What did he do **next**? Who is **last**? What did you hear **last**?
  Use the left to right sequence to teach and reinforce **before** and **after**.
  Use the same sequence to encourage prediction.

Class 11

Coping in groups

Children with ASD have poor social communication skills – they may seem barely aware that they are part of a class, and some do not seem to acknowledge the presence of others even when they are part of a small group at the same table. Many children are overwhelmed by being with others because of conversational noise, movement of people, clothing etc. They may have poor conversation and social interaction skills and find it difficult to single out people as separate, unique identities.

They may find it difficult to share jokes because this involves understanding others' viewpoints, something slow to develop in children with ASD.

Some situations may cause particular difficulties such as being in groups in the hall, lunchtimes and playtimes (see Ch. 1, Assemblies, Playtimes and Lunchtimes for advice on supporting these children in those contexts).

Strategies

- Reinforce small group identity. Preface instructions, for example: 'Blue group, you can go first.' A variation of 'Simon says' can be played using the names of the class groups instead of 'Simon', as in 'Blue group stand up. Red group touch your toes.' The group lose a point if they do the wrong thing. Allow the child time to copy the others. Reinforce class identity with displays of class photos, lists of names and birthdays.
- Teach the child the names of children in the class, starting with his group.
- When the child knows a few children by name, see if he can find out and remember anything about them – if they have brothers or sisters, their favourite food, toy, television programme etc. More ideas to encourage interaction can be found in the social filing cabinet in Section 2.

Suggestions for IEP targets

These should be Specific, Measurable, Achievable, Relevant, Timed (i.e. **SMART**).

Inevitably behaviour targets are going to be very specific for each child – it is not possible to make them universally relevant. However, the following may prove helpful as a guide.

Desired behaviour **For (*name of child*) to:**	**Suggested strategy** **(specify reward system)**
ask adult for help using help card (*where/when*)	social story practise help card strategy
stay in (*define area*) at *playtimes/lunchtimes*	social story reward system
stay with (*name people*) at *playtime/lunchtimes*	buddy system play pals (*specify who*)
eat all food in lunchbox	liaise with home social story reward system picture sequence
to sit in designated place at *lunchtime/carpet time*	social story rehearsal special seat/carpet tile
wait/take turns in queue	agree position role play use prompt card social story
behave appropriately in assembly for (*specify*) minutes	social story reward system
take turns appropriately (*when/where*)	social story role play reward system
learn and follow 'carpet time rules'	role play social story reward system rules on display
use prompt card as agreed before angry outburst	role play social story reward system

Desired behaviour For (*name of child*) to:	Suggested strategy (specify reward system)
join in circle *time/assembly* appropriately	social story reward system
keep talk about (*his obsession*) to agreed times	social story reward system talk ticket
reduce incidents of (*specify e.g. making noises*) to (*specify*)	social story star chart
attend appropriately for (*x*) minutes in (*setting*)	social story star chart reward system
put up his hand and wait before speaking	talk ticket social story reward system
make more appropriate eye contact by looking at mouth/ear/chin for X % of the time (*specify*)	play eye contact games social story
know names of (*specify*) children in group	introduce one child at a time in games refer to new child often encourage use of name after modelling
reduce number of tantrums by X % (*specify*)	keep incident record use visual schedule to avoid sudden changes social story reward system
follow timetable	visual schedule transition planner prompt card buddy system
bring correct equipment (*specify*) to *school/class*	visual schedule transition planner colour coding personal equipment liaise and send home equipment lists use organisation framework buddy system

Chapter 2: Thinking and learning

Learning 1

Seeing the bigger picture

Children with ASD seem to have difficulty integrating what they know and see to form 'the bigger picture'. All the individual parts are recognised but not pieced together to give an overall meaning. For instance, if told that a doctor, lawyer and priest visited an old man in that order, a pupil with ASD would not necessarily understand that the man had died.

Sometimes a child picks up on details that cloud understanding or which distract him. For instance, a child with ASD saw a video of *The Railway Children*, and understood it to be about railways. He remembered all the trains, bridges, viaducts and track but did not understand what the story was about. A younger child could not understand about farming because he was only interested in learning the animals' names. Another could not recall the names of the animals because he was only interested in the farm machinery.

Some children find it hard to connect pieces of information and may also lack flexibility in their thinking. They may have difficulty generalising learning from one situation to another. Others may rigidly apply what they have learned to another situation but without the flexibility to respond to the differences. For example, a child was told a story about an animal called Barney who liked to play and fetch sticks in the park – he refused to believe the animal was not a dinosaur because it was called Barney (from the cartoon *The Flintstones*), in spite of the evidence to the contrary. Another child could 'take away' but not 'subtract' when he moved to a different school.

Difficulties such as these affect how well a child can use his intellectual skills.

Strategies

- Demonstrate how new material relates to something learned earlier. Supplement this with questions which will help him to link the new information to something you know he has learned.
- Make activities meaningful by building on his likes, interests and strengths.
- Some of his learning experiences should be co-operative rather than entirely instructional.
- Tell the child when two situations are similar then ask him to tell you what is the same and different about them.
- Use text and pictures to provide visual support as he thinks. This will also make him look again for cues or details he may have missed.
- Use specially designed materials to help the child collect information and integrate it to create new meaning (see Section 4, Resources).
- Use mindmaps to show connections between concepts and topics.

Learning 2

Single channel focus

As previously stated, many children with ASD find it difficult to take in information through more than one channel; they may listen or look but not both at the same time as this may cause overload. Touching the child at the same time as talking to him may distract him from what you are saying because of the additional sensory input. Multitasking such as listening and taking notes simultaneously is difficult.

Children with ASD seem to process language differently to others; many seem to need extra time to decode what they hear before they can respond to the meaning, rather like conversing in an unfamiliar foreign language. They may not be able to concentrate on the picture, music etc. all at the same time.

Some children's sense perceptions are extremely acute; uninvited and unexpected touching may be experienced as pain.

Strategies

- Say the child's name to gain his attention before giving an instruction.
- Use exactly the same words if you need to repeat an instruction or the child may think he has been given a second, different instruction.
- Use visual support for the child to refer to when you have stopped talking and he has stopped listening. Pointing and speaking at the same time may confuse him. Allow time for him to hear what you have to say then look at the illustration.
- Give him handouts to summarise your main points instead of expecting him to make notes as you speak.
- Use flow diagrams to emphasise key information.
- Don't ask him to do more than one thing at once.
- Keep classroom distractions to a minimum.
- Use a neutral tone without emotional content to avoid distracting him from the content.
- Use a work station to reduce visual distractions (see Section 2, Setting up a work station).
- Do not emphasise eye contact as this may limit his understanding.

Learning 3

Homework

Homework is intended to support the learning in school. In the case of pupils with ASD the usual set homework may not be appropriate or supportive of school learning.

Homework can be a considerable source of distress to the pupil and his family, resulting in difficult relationships between home and school. For homework to be successful it must have an achievable and desirable outcome, i.e. the pupil will be capable of doing it and will learn something from it. School staff should be made aware if a parent is able or willing to help or supervise so that the homework can be set accordingly. It is important for staff to know whether the homework will be done independently or with support.

Some pupils with ASD bitterly resent doing school work at home because it impinges on opportunities to pursue their own interests and they may not see the point – their understanding is that school is for school work and home is for non-school work. Often, pupils don't seem to know what they are supposed to be doing and do not take home the necessary equipment. They may also have organisational difficulties such as problems planning and organising their time.

Strategies

- Decide with the pupil's family whether it would be better to have no homework, supervised homework or independent homework, for how long and on which nights.
- Agree a homework contract between home, pupil and school and review it frequently.
- Make homework enjoyable, i.e. something at which the pupil can succeed.
- Homework should be relevant.
- Set tasks which extend the child's understanding of himself such as finding things out about his own family, his family history and constructing his own personal timeline of events which are significant to him.
- Set tasks which involve communicating with home about what has happened at school and vice versa (for suggestions see Section 2, Home/school liaison).
- Use homework to prepare the child for new topics and changes that will affect him such as preparing for a school trip. He could read about a subject before embarking on its study.
- Work together to ensure the pupil knows what he has to do, what he needs and when he should pack it. Consider using other children to check his homework diary to make sure he has everything he needs (see Ch. 1, Organisation and Section 2, Using a buddy system/Organisation strategies).
- Consider setting up a homework club after school or at lunchtime. Access to resources such as the library would avoid the need to take books home and also reduce pressure at home.

Learning 4

Independence

Pupils with ASD are not very independent learners; they rely heavily on others to structure their environment and give them clear directions about what they are to do. Self-monitoring is problematical – pupils may not have the necessary resolve and self-discipline to stick at a task or to know when they are finished and if they are successful. They need clear feedback on their progress.

Their organisational difficulties mean they cannot plan because they are unable to mentally project a picture of themselves and what they will need in preparation. Their lack of flexibility and imagination also affects how effective they are in learning independently because they do not easily make links between new and previously learned information.

Because these children do not easily transfer what they have learned from one situation to another similar, but not identical, situation, they may find it difficult to apply the skills they have already acquired.

Attention skills may also be an issue – it is difficult to be independent when you can't start or stay on a task by yourself. Each child is different and will need different strategies at different times to promote independent learning.

Strategies

- Modify the environment as much as is necessary to support independent learning. This needs to be reviewed and will change over time.
- Establish routines and structures for each day (see Section 2, Visual schedules and transition planners).
- Teach school and class rules, as well as the 'rules' for each activity.
- Organise books and equipment so the child knows where everything is. Make sure there is enough locker space and colour code if helpful (see Ch. 1, Organisation and Section 2, Organisation strategies).
- The physical space in the classroom should include places for the child to work at different activities and may include a work station (see Ch. 1, Boundaries and Section 2, Setting up a work station).
- Identify the child's individual pattern of difficulties and determine strategies to help with specifics.
- With the child, set IEP targets if appropriate and support with a reward system or social story.
- Liaise with home if appropriate to maintain a consistent approach to meeting his needs.

Attention 1

Listening

Listening may be impaired in children with ASD because of their distractibility (for a range of reasons both internal and external – see Ch. 1, Distractibility and Ch. 5, Following instructions).

Optimum conditions for listening need to be created, for example having a special place and learning what to do in order to listen properly, i.e.:

- look at the teacher;
- listen carefully;
- keep quiet;
- sit still (see Ch. 1, Carpet time).

The language used with the child needs to be appropriate for his level of understanding. The vocabulary and sentence grammar, as well as length and complexity of what is said, must match the child's receptive language abilities. Brighter children with ASD may appear to have better receptive language skills than they have in reality because they may use very adult words.

The child may have a poor auditory memory for sequences which will impair the quantity of information he can take in and recall. Children with ASD tend to take things literally. They may not understand idioms and will not therefore make the expected inferences; as a result they become confused and stop listening.

Strategies

- Use the child's name to gain his attention before giving instructions and use it from time to time to regain his attention (see Ch. 1, Carpet time).
- Give the child a purpose for listening.
- Keep language simple and within his understanding.
- Keep language direct and avoid using inference, metaphors and figures of speech if possible; where necessary, explain them (see Ch. 5, Literal understanding/Inference).
- Teach him that listening involves keeping his mind on the same thing as the speaker. Give him something to hold which may help to keep his mind on the subject, such as a picture or object relating to the topic under discussion.
- Negotiate time for the child to talk about his special interest if preoccupation with this interferes with his listening.
- Give the child time to process one piece of information before moving on – some children can take up to seven seconds.
- Use circle time activities to promote listening.
- Provide a social story about listening, specific to the child and his situation.
- Modify the environment to remove possibilities of distraction:
     Don't sit him by noisy heaters and busy areas.
     Keep him away from children who are likely to distract him.
     Cover up objects which distract him such as computer screens.
     Let him sit in a special quiet place to listen if it helps.

Attention 2

Starting a task

This can prove quite problematical for some children with ASD for several reasons:

- He did not pay attention because he was distracted or daydreaming.
- He has a poor attention span.
- He has difficulty understanding the vocabulary and/or sentence structure used.
- He is slow to process language and has missed parts of the instruction.
- He has a poor auditory memory for sequences – he can't remember what he has been told.
- He cannot understand non-literal language such as inference, humour and figures of speech.
- He has a misinterpreted due to his own idea of how things should be done.
- He has a lack of planning and organisation skills make it difficult for him to visualise the end of the task and plan the steps he needs to take, in particular the first step.
- He has never started on his own, depending entirely on help.
- He habitually refuses or ignores requests to get started.
- He has an expectation that he will not be able to perform the task to his own exacting standards so he avoids failure by not starting at all.

Strategies

- Work out what is happening from the child's point of view. Note the sequence of events when he does not get started, for example what happens between giving the instruction and starting the task:

    Does the child have to move or get equipment?

    Is there a memory/attention difficulty? Does the child behave in the same way when starting all tasks?

    Why is he more successful in one situation than another, for instance does the teacher/subject/length of instruction/language used/room/position in room/other pupils/proximity of other pupils/distractions etc. have anything to do with his response?

    How do you know he understands what he has to do?

- Use this information to make positive changes in his environment, your approach and expectations.
- Use visual strategies to help him organise what he has to do such as task cards, diagrams, bullet points, mindmaps, storylines and flowcharts.
- Teach him about draft and finished work if this is an issue, and help him understand that a first draft is not and should not be perfect. Use a social story to support this.
- Use a social story to target and change specific behaviour such as to:

    plan the activity using a storyline (see Section 2, Organisation strategies);

    pick up his pencil when asked;

    repeat an instruction.

- Use a timer to start (as well as maintain) an activity.

Attention 3

Staying on task

Many children – not just those with ASD – have difficulties staying on task. Their attention span may be short in comparison with others of the same age. They appear not to be able to remember for long what they are supposed to be doing.

Some children who have difficulty staying on task may also be hyperactive, as in those with attention deficit hyperactivity disorder (ADHD). Others may be able to stay on a task of their own choosing but have difficulty with a teacher-directed task, perhaps because they find it too challenging, not interesting, not relevant, not their own agenda or they are unable to do it on their own terms.

Often a degree of self-monitoring is required which children with ASD and younger children may not have. In these cases, the child will be dependent on others to prompt and encourage him to keep on task.

Children who have difficulty staying on task do not deliberately forget what they are supposed to be doing and are not being naughty – they are unaware they are off task until they are told. However, they can be helped to stay on task and their self-monitoring skills improved.

Strategies

- Observe how long the child stays on task. Note variations and which factors seem to be helping him stay on task for longer and which factors distract him. Notice the nature of the task, how well he was prepared as well as other factors in the environment which may help or hinder him. Use this information to create optimum conditions to help him stay on task.

- Extend the time on task by setting time targets such as 20 seconds or one minute beyond his usual concentration span (you can use a timer). Reward achievement of the new time.

- Help the child to organise what he can do in an agreed time such as three sentences or four sums and then extend this as appropriate.

- Use visual support to help him remember what he has to do and to remind him to return to task (such as a card on the table with '3 sums' written on it). Provide a picture and reward to remind him.

- Agree the time on task with the child and make this an IEP target.

- Other strategies can be found in Chapter 1 (Organisation) and Chapter 2 (Independence).

Attention 4

Fatigue

The effort of having to work out what is expected in behaviour, learning, interacting and understanding as well as trying to conform to these expectations can be exhausting. It is relatively common for many children with ASD to have significant sleep problems which can mean that they are very tired at school. Tired children cannot tolerate stress well and their behaviour can deteriorate. They may find it harder to stay on task and are less likely to be able to cope with any upset or change; they may become angry, irritated and intolerant with very little provocation.

Some children with ASD have eating and/or bowel problems. If they have not eaten breakfast before they come to school, they may become very hungry and perhaps irritable or may seem sluggish and tired.

Although you may not be able to do anything about the fatigue as such, you may be able to help remove additional stresses and assist the child to develop strategies to cope.

Strategies

- Allow the child a small snack at fruit time, especially if he does not eat breakfast or dislikes fruit.
- A visual schedule, such as photographs of the sequence of food to be eaten, may be necessary to encourage the child to eat enough lunch if this is an issue.
- Use a home/school book or other way of liaising with parents so that you know when and why the child is tired or upset (see Section 2, Home/school liaison).
- If the child is obviously very tired, reduce or change your expectations for the lesson or part of the day.
- Organise a 'safe base' within or outside of the classroom where the child can go if he is not coping.
- Notice 'early warning' symptoms and use 'time out' to avert difficulties of which the child may not be aware.
- Be consistent and prepare the child for changes if they cannot be avoided.
- If the fatigue results in deteriorating behaviour, see Chapter 1 for areas which will be affected and strategies to try.

Thinking 1

Rigidity of thought

Rigid thinking is typical of children with ASD – they do not readily modify their original opinion or judgement in the light of further information. This can make them inflexible in their approach to many learning situations. For example, a child may have great difficulty coming to terms with the variety of ways of doing subtraction.

This can also cause social interaction problems because a characteristic of ASD is the inability (or difficulty) to 'mind read', i.e. understand that others have different opinions, motivations and experiences equally valid to their own. Because they do not see things from the point of view of others, the only interpretation of an event is their own. As a consequence these children lack an understanding of others' needs and ideas. A pupil with ASD cannot make fine adjustments in his understanding and response to others – he will try to impose his own views on others and cannot readily adapt or see that some things may be relative.

Flexibility of thought requires imagination, and pupils with ASD generally have poor imaginations. It may be necessary to challenge in order to extend or change a pupil's point of view but this should be done in a manner which does not provoke insecurities that will give rise to control issues and even more rigid thinking.

Strategies

- Use a neutral and unemotional tone when challenging your pupil's thinking, and be as non-confrontational as possible. Sit side by side, not in front of him.

- Use diagrams, mindmaps and comic strip cartoons to illustrate other people's points of view and other possible outcomes. See Carol Gray's *Comic Strip Conversations* (Section 4, Resources).

- Use role play to help him understand other viewpoints. The same scene could be played several times with the child playing a different character each time.

Thinking 2

Fact, fiction and imagination

It is generally observed that children with ASD have difficulties with the development of play and imaginative thinking, probably because they find it difficult to see things from a different point of view. The concept of pretence is problematical and they may sometimes think that another place or time is real.

Some children believe that dinosaurs still exist and don't really understand that Thomas the Tank Engine is fictional, long after other children their age have worked this out. Some children cannot differentiate fact from fiction and make up things without being aware that they have done so – it is as if the memory of what they have thought or said is as strong as the memory of what they have seen, heard or done. Once expressed verbally it seems to become a fact as far as these children are concerned. They do not think they are lying and can become quite upset if they are challenged.

Some children seem unable to separate fact from fiction even when they know the difference. Lying involves attempting to deliberately manipulate someone else's belief system usually in order to avoid a consequence. In general, younger children with ASD do this much less than other children probably because they have poorly developed 'mind-reading' skills. They need to know another's point of view in order to manipulate it and this is a genuinely weak area in children with ASD. However, some older children, having 'learned' to lie, are often caught out because they are not very skilled liars.

Most children with ASD prefer to stick to the rules as they understand them and are less likely than other children to attempt to avoid consequences.

Strategies

- Use text such as stories and videos to talk about what is real/not real. Talk about how stories and characters are created and encourage the child to make up a story and characters for himself.
- In the case of a child who cannot separate fact from fiction, make a timeline of his life and refer to it when deciding if an event really happened. Ask how old he was, which house he lived in, who was there, etc.
- Liaise with his family so that you know what is happening outside school and then you can check facts.
- Use two boxes, one for things which are true, one for things which are made up. Write/draw any incidents reported, then decide which box it should go into.
- Use mindmaps to illustrate the importance (and hierarchy) of ideas, facts or information.

Thinking 3

Thinking skills

Thinking is a skill. Thinking is what you do when you see a connection between things and ideas. When you can see a relationship between things you haven't seen before, you have a new understanding and a new meaning. It is something you have to do for yourself.

Some of the thinking skills most affected by ASD are:

- Sequencing, needed to understand cause and effect, follow instructions, understand time, reading and number work. Many children with ASD find sequencing difficult.

- Knowing about positions in space and understanding them both physically and metaphorically. This skill helps you to recognise relationships, as in science and technology, but also helps you to understand other points of view, as in, 'I see where you are coming from ...' 'From where I stand ...' This can be very difficult for pupils with ASD.

- Being able to make a hypothesis and modify it – many pupils with ASD stick rigidly to their first idea.

- Thinking about more than one thing at a time, which people with ASD find difficult, particularly when they have a single channelled approach.

- Knowing what is important, how to prioritise, what is relevant and what is redundant. Pupils with ASD find this difficult. If they can't see the bigger picture and become distracted by details they will find it very hard to prioritise and decide what is relevant and redundant.

Pupils with ASD need help to develop these skills so that they can use them for themselves.

Strategies

- Encourage the pupil to make his own connections. Ask questions but do not do it for him unless it is necessary, and then check that he can follow the connection.

- Encourage the pupil to use illustrations and diagrams in books to aid his comprehension.

- Ask him to repeat the line he has just read or the gist of what you have just said.

- Encourage prediction both in relation to what he sees, as in actions, events and in his reading, as well as to what he hears from others.

- Give the pupil non-fiction books when teaching him to retrieve information. He is likely to prefer realism to fantasy although he should be allowed access to a variety of reading material.

- Use opportunities to talk about what factors are more important in particular situations. For instance, when it snows ask if it is more important to wear a hat or a tee shirt/ to wear a red or black coat/to have hot food or cold food/to have a sledge or football/ to have a cat or a dog, etc.

- Use published materials to practise these thinking skills (see Section 4, Resources).

Thinking 4

Mind reading

Babies do not see others as separate from themselves – one crying baby can set off all the babies in a nursery. They have no sense of boundaries. As toddlers they discover that people have separate bodies but they have yet to learn that others have thoughts and feelings separate from their own.

The next step is to understand that others have separate emotions. It takes until they are about six years old before children understand that other people have separate thoughts of their own. Children with ASD learn how to mind read much later than other children and will continue to be less skilled in this area throughout life.

Mind reading is necessary for:

- forming friendships;
- understanding non-verbal communication such as body language, facial expression, tone of voice;
- motivating and leading others;
- manipulating others;
- avoiding hurting others' feelings.

It is considered an essential skill for human development.

Strategies

- Encourage symbolic play in young children in which one thing stands for another, such as a box representing a car.
- Encourage pretend play in which the child pretends to be someone else and plays out a situation, perhaps in the home corner. This is hard for children with ASD who are more likely to play at being animals and make noises. They may need to be shown what to do.
- Interactive play with another child should be encouraged so there are opportunities for social play as well as role play. Starting initially with one child, at first you will need to support turntaking. Increase the number of children in the group, still supporting turntaking. Try using a talk ticket which each child holds when it is their turn.
- Encourage play which enables and practises understanding of how others feel, such as pretending to be angry, sad, frightened etc.
- Use circle time games to encourage awareness of non-verbal cues such as facial expression, listening and acting out scenes.
- Talk about others' feelings and thoughts as they arise. Encourage the child to notice how he knows that the other child is upset – refer to facial expression, tone of voice and body language.
- Use toys and games to encourage the child to think about feelings and their expression (see Section 4, Resources).

Suggestions for IEP targets

These should be Specific, Measurable, Achievable, Relevant, Timed (i.e. **SMART**).

   Inevitably targets are going to be very specific for each child and it is not possible – it is not possible to make them universally relevant. However, the following may prove helpful as a guide.

Desired behaviour For (*name of child*) to:	Suggested strategy (specify reward system)
relate new information to something learned earlier X % of the time (*specify*)	use questioning use resources (*specify e.g.* *prepared worksheets*)

follow class routines	use visual schedules/transition
	   planners
	learn and display rules
	encourage child to repeat
	   instructions

work at *designated area/* *work station* appropriately	set up work station teach procedures

do agreed homework	contract between
	   home/school/child
	make sure child has written it
	   down and has correct equipment

organise equipment for home	*buddy/teacher* to check equipment at end of day

do and bring in homework	contract between
	   parents/school/child
	home/school liaison record
	   forms
	social story

reduce distractibility in
class/carpet time/assembly
	describe planned changes e.g.
	   limit listening time,
	   seat in different place, etc.

improve *willingness to* *listen/length of time listening*	use reward system social story circle time activities

Desired behaviour For (*name of child*) to:	Suggested strategy (specify reward system)
start a task following instructions X % of the time (*specify*)	use a *mindmap/storyline* social story reward system
stay on task for __ minutes (*specify*)	use visual cues (*specify*) use timer use storyline reward system

Chapter 3: Conversation skills

Verbal 1

Listener knowledge and listener needs

In a satisfactory conversation all the speakers need to be aware of the knowledge being shared. When knowledge is not shared, listeners need more information so they know what, when, to whom or to which setting the speaker is referring.

Young children often assume that if they know something you also share this knowledge – that you know where they live, who their relations are and their past history. They slowly learn that other people's knowledge is different to theirs and that others see things differently from them. Known as the 'theory of mind', by the age of six most children will have developed this ability.

However, development is much slower in children with ASD and some may never fully develop this skill – they are likely to continue to assume that their knowledge is shared by others. They do not easily recognise the validity of other children's responses and are not interested in their thoughts and activities unless they correspond with their own.

These difficulties are very apparent in conversation. Because they do not know what others need to know, children with ASD may either give too much information or not enough. Insufficient information can lead to a breakdown in understanding but because these children do not recognise this they may become frustrated and angry at what, in their view, is the fault of the listener.

Children with ASD may not fully understand a conversation that includes non-verbal messaging: for example when conversation is accompanied by shrugging, rolling the eyes, grimacing; when the tone of voice intensifies or suggests an alternative meaning to the words; and when references are hinted at and not made explicit.

Strategies

- Note when conversational breakdown occurs and encourage the child to reflect on the reason why. Ask him what he needs to say to make others understand him and tell him (gently) if necessary.

- Encourage him to think of the 'wh' words when he is talking to others. They need to know **wh**en, **wh**ere, **wh**o and **wh**at he is talking about. Ask him to reflect on what has **not** been said when misunderstandings occur.

- Help him to understand that others have different points of view dependent on what they know and have learned from their experience. For example, another child may not have the same depth of knowledge of the solar system/computers/battles, for example, so will require more information in order to be able to fully understand.

- Encourage him to ask for further explanation if he does not understand, and to provide more information if he is asked without getting cross.

- Model an unclear message and encourage the child to correct it so it can be understood.

- Use storylines (see Section 2, Organisation strategies) and mindmaps to plan spoken and written language activities.

Verbal 2

Turntaking

Children with ASD are often not good at turntaking because:

- they may have a desire to express their own thoughts and ideas which are of great interest to them, but conversely may show little interest in others' contributions;
- they lack the skills necessary to maintain conversations;
- they do not recognise the non-verbal cues necessary to maintain a conversation;
- they may have poor listening or auditory memory skills.

A child who is not interested in what others have to say may try to control the conversation by speaking at length on his choice of subject. He may be unaware that others are bored and have lost interest, and may ignore their contributions. He may have difficulty maintaining interest in a topic chosen by someone else and may try to bring the conversation back to his topic rather than let it flow naturally.

Children with poor conversation skills may not know how to join a conversation appropriately and their timing may be poor. They may not know how to let others in. They may be unaware of the to-and-fro nature of turntaking and may not know how long a turn takes.

Their difficulties in picking up on non-verbal communication such as tone of voice, facial expression and body language are contributory factors to their lack of skill at turntaking (see non-verbal cues in this chapter, below).

Strategies

- Play non-verbal and verbal turntaking games (see Section 2, Activities to promote non-verbal awareness).
- Use circle time games to develop listening and turntaking.
- Use the conversation cue cards in Section 2 to determine the child's specific difficulties and to develop his awareness and skills.
- Make sure he knows how to signal to a speaker that he wants to join in and can recognise these signals from another speaker.
- Use role play with another adult to model and practise joining a conversation.
- Use role play to model what not to do. This can be useful for other children in the class who may also have difficulties for other reasons.
- Use a talk ticket or Mr Turn puppet for certain class/group discussions. Only the person holding the talk ticket or puppet may speak, but it must be passed on.
- Consider using an egg timer or something similar to limit the length of a turn.
- Discourage the child from interrupting, but also teach him that it is appropriate in an emergency and that there is a polite way to interrupt. Be explicit about when this is acceptable.
- Discuss with the children the need for rules in conversation (see Section 2,

Conversation cue cards). These rules can be displayed on a wall or put on a desk to show when they are operating. All the children should conform to the rules.

- Let the child know when he has not observed the rules but give feedback in a neutral tone of voice.

- Discuss a series of interesting pictures or objects – the children have to take turns (up to three turns each).

Verbal 3

Initiating and developing conversations

Some ASD children are socially isolated and rarely start conversations. Many have to learn how to join in and have difficulty because they have not understood the unwritten rules. They may find it difficult to develop conversations due to their poor listening and attention skills. The child's responses may be irrelevant or inappropriate to the conversation in hand.

Difficulty in developing appropriate conversation skills is often a part of the greater social communication and interaction problems that children with ASD experience. Nevertheless, these are skills which can be improved – to some extent at least.

Strategies

- Engineer situations in which the child has to approach others because you have created a need for him to do so, such as giving a message to another child or finding out some information. Model and guide to ensure it is done appropriately.

- Use circle time games to promote listening and responding to others.

- Teach the child to share information by following activities which give the children opportunities to say something about themselves, such as their special interests, their favourite food, etc. The other children can ask a question each.

- Each child can write a sentence about their own and one other child's special interest, based on what was said in the group.

- Use a social story to teach about approaching another child to talk about his interest, for instance ending with something like, 'He will like it if I talk to him about football.'

- Teach the child the rules of joining in conversations. These can be displayed on a wall as a model for all the class (see Section 2, Conversation cue cards).

- Observe the child in the playground to see where he makes mistakes joining in ongoing talk and activities. Teach joining skills, such as 'watch, listen, move close, join in'.

- Use a circle of friends (see Section 2) to help the child learn how to address and respond to different people when his responses are inappropriate.

- If possible, find out why the child's responses seem irrelevant. The difficulty may be related to the level of comprehension, perhaps because non-literal comprehension – such as the use of inference or idioms – has confused the child (see Ch. 5, Comprehension).

- Give the child sufficient processing time so that he can respond appropriately.

- Break down spoken language into smaller chunks if you suspect there may be an auditory memory difficulty contributing to apparently irrelevant responses.

Non-verbal 1

Body language and gesture

Communication is not just verbal – according to the experts, between 60% and 90% of communication is non-verbal, i.e. most meaning is conveyed through body language, gesture, facial expression and tone of voice.

Most children learn this instinctively and can recognise when someone is agitated, angry, depressed, sad, upset or hurt etc. They can often tell when someone is lying because their body language may send a different message to that of their words.

As already stated, children with ASD find it very difficult to understand non-verbal communication because it requires knowledge of how someone else is thinking or feeling when they do not feel the same – they are often unable to recognise or verbalise their own feelings, let alone anyone else's. This is one of the reasons why people with ASD are often described as being aloof, lacking in empathy and appearing emotionally detached. This is simply because they don't recognise and share others' states of mind due to their difficulty in understanding the subtle nuances of body language.

Gesture is rarely used and understood by children with ASD because it involves knowing social codes and conventions, a difficult area. However, it is worth teaching as it arises so that the child can understand and share its use by others. An example is understanding that the 'thumbs up' sign means everything is OK. Gesture is probably best taught when it replaces speech – there are many autistic children who would not understand gestures if accompanied by speech as they cannot usually multichannel (see Ch. 2, Single channel focus).

Strategies

- Write words or draw pictures of actions on cards. Give one to a child to mime, for example brushing teeth, getting dressed, stamping and posting a letter. The other children watch and name the action. This is useful to help the child see how much can be understood from looking carefully.

- Do the same with cards which show physical states, such as being tired, limping, holding their head or tummy as if suffering from a stomach ache or headache. The other children watch and name the state.

- Do the same with emotional states such as happy, sad, cross etc. These will be mimed using body language and facial expression.

- Talk about what can be understood about how people look and move in pictures and stories. Televisions and videos can be useful for this.

- Encourage the child to copy others in drama lessons to help develop his awareness of others' bodies. This can be done using a mirror image activity such as one person copying exactly what the other is doing as if in a mirror. In this activity the child has the experience of moving his own body and also seeing what it looks like through the movements of the other person.

- Teach understanding of common age-appropriate gestures so that the child is not excluded from this means of communication. Be careful and explicit in teaching where and when it is appropriate to use each gesture.

Non-verbal 2

Facial expression and eye contact

Occasionally a child with ASD will stare at others' faces inappropriately or push his own face too close, both of which make other children feel uncomfortable. He seems to find the movements of a face fascinating but may lack awareness of the whole person. Continuing to do this when he has been asked not to also shows a lack of empathy.

Most children with ASD have difficulty looking at others' faces and holding a gaze – for some this is very threatening and they feel uncomfortable. These children may also object when others stand too close to them, perhaps within touching distance, or too close to an object the child feels belongs to him.

When children do not look appropriately they may miss how the speaker feels about what he is saying, such as looking uncomfortable when lying. They are also likely to find it harder to follow class discussions when conversation flows between many speakers.

The child with ASD needs to be encouraged to keep glancing at people's faces and make eye contact, but should never be pressured to do this. How much eye contact is appropriate is to some extent culturally determined – in some countries children never make eye contact with their elders as a sign of respect. Most adults, in order to avoid seeming shifty, tend to look for several seconds at the left eye, right eye and lips for about equal amounts of time when taking part in a face-to-face conversation.

Most children with ASD tend to take in information through one channel at a time, so if they are listening they will find it distracting to look at the same time (see Ch. 2, Single channel focus). Some eye experts believe that some of these children take in information through their peripheral vision and therefore have no need to look directly.

Strategies

- Direct the child's attention to other people's faces by playing games to promote eye contact. Say why you are doing it and what he may miss if he does not look.
- If eye contact is not possible, the child might respond to looking at the lips.
- See games and activities to improve non-verbal awareness in Section 2.
- Use LDA cards or similar to help develop awareness of people's expressions.
- Use computer programs (one is available from the National Autistic Society) and a digital camera to develop awareness of facial expressions.
- Use role play, mime and drama to help develop awareness.

Non-verbal 3

Tone of voice

The tone of voice a speaker uses conveys a great deal about him and his attitude to the message and the listener. This is largely lost on children with ASD who will tend to respond to the words, taking them literally.

Most children understand sarcasm by the time they are nine years old, helped by the intonation of the speaker, but a child with ASD is likely to remain puzzled for longer. Some children consider all obscure or confusing information as a joke. Some of these children get upset when they are spoken to in an emotional tone. This can distract from how well they understand what is being said to them. Some people with ASD find emotions in others unpredictable, confusing and demanding – they know a response is required but they don't know what. Some children may interpret all emotional intonation as anger.

Children with ASD are often unable to recognise their own emotional state and are therefore likely to make mistakes trying to work out what someone else is feeling, particularly when the feeling is conveyed by the tone of voice. They are likely to be either unaware or to misinterpret the signals transmitted by the tone of someone's voice as well as their body language. Difficulty in absorbing information through more than one channel may also affect the message the child actually receives.

Strategies

- Use a neutral tone of voice when talking to the child – an emotional tone will upset and confuse him.

- Talk to him about how people's voices change according to their emotions and the message they want to convey. Practise using a happy/sad/excited tone of voice.

- Explain how messages are conveyed verbally and non-verbally, for instance showing another person that you want to join in the conversation without interrupting (see Section 2, Conversation cue cards).

- Demonstrate the different ways in which the same words can be spoken to give different meanings. Use examples such as 'I want an apple', which could be an order, impolite request or a whine; 'That is very good' could be sarcastic or congratulatory; 'This is the last meal you eat today' could be informative or threatening.

- Help the child to understand that tone of voice is only one form of non-verbal communication and that there are others. Talk about them in relation to his own experience.

- Use real examples relevant to the child to help him understand the intended subtle meaning rather than just the 'surface' meaning which the words convey.

- See Section 2 for activities to raise awareness of non-verbal communication.

Suggestions for IEP targets

These should be Specific, Measurable, Achievable, Relevant, Timed (i.e. **SMART**).

Inevitably behaviour targets are going to be very specific for each child – it is not possible to make them universally relevant. However, the following may prove helpful as a guide.

Desired behaviour For (*name of child*) to:	Suggested strategy (specify reward system)
develop awareness that others have different knowledge	use the social filing cabinet collect and record some facts about other children's likes and interests create need for child to approach others with genuine questions
supply further information without getting cross X % of the time (*specify*)	model unclear messages social story
join a conversation without *interrupting/changing to own topic*	use circle time games use conversation cue cards learn and display 'rules of conversation' model and role play
take a number of conversational turns in specified situations	use circle time games use conversation cue cards learn and display 'rules of conversation' model and role play use a 'talk ticket' to show when it is his turn or the right time to talk use timer to control length of turns social story
develop awareness of *body language/gesture/ facial expression* (*specify which one*)	model and teach use circle time games use picture cards/digital camera/computer programs use role play, drama, mime see Section 2 on games to develop non-verbal awareness

Desired behaviour For (*name of child*) to:	Suggested strategy (specify reward system)
develop more appropriate eye contact	direct attention and give reasons use role play, drama, mime play games to promote eye 　　contact – see Section 2
use/respond appropriately to tone of voice X % of the time	use circle time games use role play, drama, mime see Section 2 on games to 　　develop non-verbal awareness

Chapter 4 Sensory and motor

Undersensitivity 1

Continual movement

Some children with ASD have sensory modulation difficulties, i.e. they cannot modulate incoming sensations. In some cases they do not receive enough information and are slow to process and make sense of it. For this reason they seem to need more stimulation than most other children in order to receive information from the environment. They seem to crave more of everything and will often repeat actions and noises which appeal.

These children need to stimulate their balance system by rocking, rolling, fidgeting and continually moving or they don't know where they are in space. They may walk by sliding their feet on the floor to help their balance, and touch doors and walls as they move around.

They may lick and taste unusual items to gain more information. They love tactile experiences and like to touch and experience different surfaces and textures. Many of these children crave physical contact such as being tickled or massaged. They may rub against other people and get too close to them for their comfort.

They often like the sensation of falling and may do dangerous things such as jump from heights, e.g. from trees. They seem to require physical excitement.

Sometimes they seem to be undersensitive to the existence of other children and will walk through their activities and over them as if they did not exist. As already stated, they are poor at recognising non-verbal cues.

Strategies

- Observe the child and note the most dangerous, antisocial or inappropriate behaviour to see if more acceptable ways could be found for the child to experience the degree of stimulation he seems to need.
- Discourage at an early age what may become inappropriate touching.
- Use the knowledge that these children learn from touch. Let them handle letters and numbers, and learn from handling objects.
- Over-exaggerate tone of voice and visual stimuli. These children like a colourful, noisy and stimulating environment.
- Restrict sitting periods such as carpet time to a realistic minimum.
- Give the child something to do such as use a stress-squeezer when he is required to sit quietly (on the basis that otherwise he will do something else).
- Provide sanctioned and acceptable opportunities to move around at frequent intervals in class time. Involving the child in a Brain Gym activity (with or without the whole class) during a literacy session, for example, may help to avert trouble (see Section 4, Resources).
- Appoint the child as a monitor and give him physical tasks to tackle such as setting out the games equipment, picking up litter, tidying up and perhaps helping the caretaker.

- Use playtimes and PE to allow these children to indulge in large movement activities such as rolling and jumping.
- Use Brain Gym activities to help co-ordinate movements and gain control.
- Refer to an occupational therapist and physiotherapist for further advice.

Oversensitivity 1

Smell, touch and taste

Children who are oversensitive to their environment are deluged with sensory information which they cannot filter out. Sensations are unavoidable and may come as a shock to the child, sometimes being experienced as pain from which, naturally, the child wants to be free. These children seem to be in a continual state of fight or flight and are extremely anxious as a result. Adult autistics say that the degree of pain and discomfort is made worse by anxiety.

Some children seem obsessed by smell and experience strong likes and dislikes to the point of aversion. This can be a distraction in school because they can't help their response. Some children will not go to the toilet in school because of the smell and experience discomfort not conducive to learning. They may not like the smell of swimming baths. They may also make comments about people and their smell if it offends them – sometimes they like body smells and may follow other children about sniffing their ears, or the teacher's foot at carpet time.

These children are likely to be 'tactile defensive' or oversensitive to touch. They may like labels on clothes cut off. They often kick off their shoes or even take off clothes. Their overreaction to tactile experiences means they may not be comfortable on the carpet at carpet time. They may hate new experiences and want to avoid clay, glue or dough because they don't like sticky fingers. They may also lash out when touched by other children, and have a low tolerance to pain and minor injuries.

Oversensitive children usually have very limited tastes; they may not eat a balanced diet and are often underweight. Their parents may need to give them supplements rather than endure a daily battle over food. Their eating habits will be rigid – food may have to be set out in a certain way and eaten in the same order.

Strategies

- Be aware of the child's sensitivities. These may show as bad behaviour because he may not be able to verbalise the problem.
- If the child is sensitive to touch, don't touch him to gain his attention.
- Keep him away from situations which might cause him to lash out at other children who touch him inadvertently. He should:
    - be first or last in a queue;
    - leave the classroom first or last;
    - avoid corridors at busy times;
    - sit near the door.
- Introduce him to new experiences gradually when he is calm and on his own. The experience should be positive and without pressure. Use his obsessions, e.g. make dinosaurs out of play dough or stick pictures in a book.
- Consult with parents about what and how much is to be eaten in school.
- Be flexible. For instance, if the school has a fruit break but the child won't eat fruit, consider an alternative such as a cereal.
- Use a social story to help the child understand inappropriate comments to other people about smell.
- Try giving him a tissue impregnated with an acceptable smell for him to use as an alternative to sniffing other people, or as a reward or distraction.

Oversensitivity 2

Sight

Children who are oversensitive to what they can see become very distracted by people, movements, colour, lights, patterns and reflections. They are likely to be sensitive to fluorescent lighting and distracted by computer screens. They may be oversensitive to others looking at them. They may gaze too much at others in circle time, which can be difficult for them and may result in bad behaviour.

There can be motor co-ordination problems which will affect their involvement in PE and other areas of the curriculum. There may be difficulties learning to read because of poor depth perception, horizontal and vertical tracking. Sometimes a figure/ground difficulty can affect a child's ability to see kerbs, ledges, walls, high equipment and bars on windows so he may appear clumsy.

Some children, because of visuo-spatial difficulties, have problems with written work such as writing in a space, using appropriate size writing and setting out maths. They may also have difficulty with art, particularly with visual representation. They may have problems determining relevance and become so distracted by details that they miss the main point; not knowing where to look for the most helpful information is also a problem. Unaccustomed changes in people's appearance, such as wearing glasses or changing a hairstyle may result in lack of recognition, confusion or anger. They may show extreme reactions to environmental changes such as displays.

Visual sequencing is not easy for children with ASD – they find it difficult to remember things in order, such as the order of getting dressed and how to lay things out. They are slow to recall what they have seen and have difficulty thinking in pictures.

Strategies

- Be aware that difficult behaviour may be a result of sensory problems.
- Keep the classroom as distraction-free as possible – at the least set aside a calm area without dangling displays, bright colours, computer screens and reflective surfaces, away from low windows and busy walkways.
- Direct attention because the child may not be looking in the right place.
- Don't stand in front of windows to instruct the class to reduce external distractions and don't walk about for the same reason.
- Don't insist the child looks at the teacher to listen as this may be distracting.
- Use natural light and keep reflective surfaces away from windows.
- Help the child who has orientation difficulties by marking out boundaries in class, or provide a map or photos of the school with routes marked.
- Give the child an alternative to a whiteboard (which may be too shiny).
- Use pastel overlays if the child is sensitive to black on white and vice versa.
- Minimise the amount of information on a page.
- Refer to an occupational therapist for advice if there are fine motor difficulties (see also Section 2).
- Refer to a developmental optometrist for advice on visual perception and motor difficulties.
- Use Brain Gym (see Section 4, Resources).

Oversensitivity 3

Sound

Many children with ASD are oversensitive to sound. Autistic adults describe sounds as amplified; they cannot screen them out or select which sounds are relevant and should be listened to. Noises, such as distant tapping or a wasp outside a window can be heard at the same time at the same volume. This deluge of sound can be painful and stressful. Some children with ASD, because they cannot be selective, cope by switching off while others make more noises (like 'white sound') to drown out the rest. It is reported that the degree of discomfort is variable and that hearing levels fluctuate; these are related to stress and anxiety.

Because it can be painful, some children fear noise before it happens. Games and PE lessons present particular problems to the oversensitive child because of the nature of the sounds, the acoustics and echoes. Some children's behaviour deteriorates hours before the impending lesson because of fear and anxiety. The dining hall and assembly hall can be difficult places for a child experiencing sound oversensitivity. Listening to audiotapes, especially in the hall, may be a particularly difficult experience for a child with ASD. Classrooms present problems with the screeching sound of chairs being moved, things falling and the hum of lights. There are often external noises which distract, such as planes going overhead and lawn mowers.

Talking on the telephone can be difficult for some children because of all the competing noises. The sudden ring upsets others and they have been known to break them on purpose. Other sounds which are known to upset some oversensitive children are school bells, fire alarms, sirens, dogs and crying babies, partly because of the unpredictability of the sounds. Some children find some sounds scary and can be seen covering their ears, and some become phobic about particular sounds.

Strategies

- Give a warning of any impending noise.
- Study the child and discover which sounds cause him distress. See what he can be protected from and which sounds can be avoided.
- Create a work station or low distraction area with barriers away from windows, busy walkways, heaters and anything else which would distract him.
- Remove the child for a while from music lessons or assemblies if these prove to be a particular area of stress. Prepare carefully for gradual reintroduction for short periods at first (a social story may help).
- Keep instructions to a minimum.
- Organise a place where the child can go for 'time out' when he is not coping and before an incident.
- Be aware of how the child's tolerance fluctuates and be realistic in expectations.
- Be aware of how other senses interact with his sensitivity to sound – he may do well with visual schedules and support.

- Consider involving the child in some small group work out of class on occasion if he finds it difficult to work in class.
- Find the most appropriate place for him to listen where he can be refocused if he becomes distracted, and reward good listening.

Motor control 1

Fine and gross motor skills

Planning and executing fine and gross motor sequences is a common problem for many children with ASD. They have difficulty thinking ahead, anticipating cause and effect, predicting consequences and reflecting on the outcomes of their own behaviour.

Every time they start an activity it is like starting afresh as if it is a completely new experience. These children seem to find it hard, and take much longer than usual, to develop a 'body map', i.e. their body's memory of how to do something in time and space. They may continually bump into the same things, such as the corner of the table.

These children need many more repetitions than usual in order to learn sequences of activities; their brains seem to find it difficult to retain these sort of memories. They often make associated movements, such as sticking their tongue out while trying to concentrate, or flapping hands while running. They may have perseverance difficulties, i.e. they find it hard to finish one task and move on to another. They often have difficulties crossing their midline which indicates a lack of integration between the sides of the brain. This has consequences in school as it is likely to affect reading and writing. It may also mean that information does not pass easily from one side of the brain to the other, resulting in rigid thinking and an inability to multitask. These children are also often slow to develop a dominant handedness.

Fine motor control difficulties affect much of home and school life, and can have a negative affect on self-esteem. Gross motor control difficulties also affect school life – children with noticeable difficulties with motor skills (whether or not they have ASD) are often easy targets for bullies.

Strategies

- Refer the child for a joint occupational therapy and physiotherapy assessment for advice and intervention.
- Include recommended activities in PE lessons, or within school hours, particularly if there are difficulties at home which prevent the child from carrying out the exercises properly.
- Start a group and carry out exercises together for 10–15 minutes daily – many children, not just those with ASD, will benefit from these exercises (see *Developmental Dyspraxia* by Madeleine Portwood, Section 4, Resources).
- Use Brain Gym movements with the whole class prior to different learning tasks (see Section 4, Resources).
- See Section 2 for more detailed strategies to help the child who requires assistance with fine and gross motor activities including dressing and handwriting.

Motor control 2

PE and games

PE and games can be problematical and distressing for children with both ASD and motor and sensory difficulties. The unpredictability of lessons may cause great anxiety.

The changed acoustics cause many children anguish, particularly those who are sensitive to noise. Whistles can be especially traumatic because they are sudden and piercing. Those who are oversensitive to movement may be similarly distressed or distracted because of the randomness of the movements of people in the room.

Children who have social interaction difficulties often find it hard to work in pairs or be part of a team. As mentioned in Chapter 3, turntaking is a problem for most children with ASD. They may have difficulty understanding, interpreting or caring about the rules of games. These children may become scapegoats if the team loses, especially if they have motor co-ordination problems and/or poor ball skills. A common cause of distress is being the last one chosen for a team.

Activities in PE usually require doing more than one thing at once, as in running and bouncing the ball at the same time, which children with ASD find almost impossible. Because they find it hard to multichannel, doing an activity while trying to follow an instruction will be very difficult and they may well not hear the instruction. Some children with ASD are bad losers and blame everyone else – they find it hard to accept that they have lost and may retaliate with aggression.

PE can be the cause of overexcitement in some children, especially those with sensory impairment such as the undersensitive. Those children with ASD who do not usually watch others in order to follow instructions may be doing (and learning) the wrong thing, not practising the desired skill and possibly putting themselves or others in danger; those who are easily led may copy dangerous behaviour.

In addition, there are all the problems associated with changing, including showering, dressing, noise, banter and horseplay of a changing room. Some children are known to be so anxious about this that they avoid school on those days.

Strategies

- Ensure changing rooms are properly supervised and there is no bullying.
- Prepare the child for PE lessons so he knows what to expect. This will involve liaising with whoever is teaching the PE lesson.
- Provide support for the child who has difficulties with some physical tasks such as balancing/social interaction/ following instructions/joining in team games at a level appropriate for his age.
- An adult who knows the child should observe and interpret the child's behaviour in PE and on PE days in the light of his difficulties. Keep a log.
- Offer alternative activities which build on individual skills such as running and working out in the gym (while the others play team games) in a small group and with an additional adult to differentiate, supervise and support. Other individual activities could include: rock climbing, golf, yoga, martial arts.

Suggestions for IEP targets

These should be Specific, Measurable, Achievable, Relevant, Timed (i.e. **SMART**).

Inevitably targets are going to be very specific for each child – it is not possible to make them universally relevant. Check if the child is undersensitive (US) or oversensitive (OS) before selecting the targets. Here are some which may prove helpful as a guide.

Desired behaviour **For (*name of child*) to:**	**Suggested strategy** **(specify reward system)**
(US) learn appropriate touching	social filing cabinet social story reward system
(OS) decrease instances of antisocial (*specify*) smelling	social story reward with alternative smells, e.g. rubbers, pens
(OS) eat what is in his lunchbox	provide sequence in words or pictures of what he has to eat
(OS) decrease sensitivity to *being touched/touching*	introduce in play situations use special interest reward system
(OS) cope better with classroom noise in specified situations for X% of the time	work station ear muffs reward system periods of time out
develop socially acceptable behaviour (*specify*)	reward system distraction technique Brain Gym social story
plan an activity	make a mindmap picture/symbol sequence
develop greater awareness of danger	pictures of cause and effect sequencing activities social story
develop better fine motor control activity (*specify*)	use OT programme Brain Gym school group
develop better gross motor skills (*specify*)	use physio programme Brain Gym structured playtime activities with (*specify*)

Chapter 5: Language and communication

Use 1

Restricted interests

Everyone is interested in subjects which give them pleasure. The enjoyment may be the result of a challenge which brings new experiences and provides the opportunity to extend skills or it may derive from being with people who share your interests as in team activities and clubs. You need to find the activity intrinsically satisfying and rewarding – people generally do not indulge in those activities they find hard for fun. For example, only those children who find them easy will do jigsaws – those who find them difficult or do not see the point will not choose this particular activity.

The interests of children with ASD need to be viewed in the same way. They are not going to find pleasure in doing things they find hard or unrewarding. They will only choose those interests which give them intrinsic satisfaction and these are unlikely to involve social interaction, sensitivity and empathy.

Children with ASD gain most pleasure from clearly defined and structured activities, often involving putting things in order and with predictable outcomes. They are also likely to repeat the same activity constantly as a means of counteracting the levels of stress induced by doing so many activities imposed upon them in school; these interests can turn into obsessions, occupying them for long periods of time often at the expense of other learning opportunities (see Ch. 1, Obsessions).

Strategies

- Some other children may have similar or overlapping interests as the ASD child. Try to persuade him to accept and allow one or two others to be included on occasion.
- Arrange times when all the children can talk about their special interest to the class, including the child with ASD.
- Allow him time to follow his interest but not to the exclusion of other possible interests.
- Try to use his special interest to develop skills which could involve others in some way, such as collecting information, asking questions and listening to and recording the answers.
- Promote other skills related to his interest such as research and IT skills.
- Acknowledge his expertise in his special area but try not to allow it to become the most important thing in his life.

Use 2

Language development

Some children with ASD do not develop language in the usual way. Others, usually those with a diagnosis of Asperger's syndrome, do not have a history of early language delay.

Pre-school children who experience significant language delay should be known to speech and language therapy services via the health visitor or the family GP; they may also be known to the Portage service which works with pre-school children at home who have various sorts of disabilities. The intervention of these services will be at a level deemed appropriate by that service.

Approaches used to encourage meaningful interaction in nursery include signing (usually Makaton) and PECS (**P**icture **E**xchange **C**ommunication **S**ystem). Speech and language therapy services provide courses for parents such as the Hanen course, *More than Words*, which supports and informs parents helping their children develop better communication and language skills.

Children with ASD often have some difficulty understanding and using pronouns in their early language development. They may use *he/she* and *him/her* interchangeably. A child may have difficulty understanding when to use *I, my* and *mine* because he is addressed by other people as *you*. This is probably linked to difficulties in seeing things from other points of view. The child finds it hard to be *you* and *I* at the same time, depending on who is speaking, and may avoid this difficulty by referring to himself by name as in '*Michael go home now.*'

Apart from this difficulty with pronouns, the child's language should follow a normal developmental pattern in line with his level of ability and in relation to the degree of impairment in his desire and ability to interact with others using language.

Strategies

- Seek advice from language professionals or from written resources (see Section 4, Resources) to help the child extend his understanding and use of vocabulary and sentence grammar.
- Extend the child's need to use language by not speaking for him or supplying answers. Play games with him such as 'What am I?' and, if he is willing, barrier games with another child (see Section 4, Resources).
- Gradually extend the range of settings in which the child will communicate.
- Use the child's special interest to extend his language uses.

Use 3

Unusual language features

Some young children with ASD 'echo' the last few words of what others say to them. This is called 'echolalia'. It may be because the children know a response is expected but don't know what or how; it can also be a result of anxiety when attention is placed on the sounds in the words rather than on their meaning.

Some young children tend to speak in fairly stereotyped language using learned phrases and sentences. This may mask difficulties the child has in generating and speaking novel sentences. It means that the pattern for the conversation is predictable.

Sometimes the child uses 'tag' questions at the end of statements such as *'isn't it?'* or *'don't I?'* which reflects his way of controlling the response. Children with ASD may use continual questions related to their special interests – these are not due to genuine curiosity but reflect a desire to control the conversation. Sometimes the same questions demanding exactly the same answers are repeated again and again. This is very clear when the questions are about events which have yet to happen and are indicative of the child's anxiety levels.

Adults often remark on the style of speech of some children with ASD because their spoken language is fairly formal and sounds pedantic. Some of the grammatical structures used are more commonly found in formal written language which is perhaps where the child may have come across them; the language sounds odd coming from a child. He may also use a slightly unusual vocabulary which is a little precise and old-fashioned.

The child may converse with adults as if he is equally adult and has the same rights and terms of address. This often reflects unawareness of appropriate social distance and distinctions, and can make the child appear rude and arrogant.

Strategies

- When the child is echolalic, try to find the reason for the anxiety and allay it (see Ch. 1, Anxiety).

- Similarly reduce stress if the child asks continual questions for reassurance. Answer him completely at first, but then only remind him of what you said previously.

- When the child asks continual questions about his obsessive interests create times when he is allowed to do this but don't go beyond those times.

- Set a target on his IEP if this is a behaviour which is a priority for change. Use a social story to support this (see Section 2).

- If it is necessary and relevant, talk to the child about appropriate conversational behaviour with different people. Use a circle of friends and the social filing cabinet (see Section 2).

- Try to raise others' awareness of the child's difficulties if they feel offended by his apparent rudeness and arrogance. In many cases the conversational behaviour will not seem so out of place when the child does reach adulthood.

Comprehension 1

Literal understanding

Children with ASD tend to take things literally, responding mainly to the surface features of language. They are unable to comprehend the real meaning and as a result may become confused or totally misunderstand.

They have particular difficulties understanding subtleties in our language. They may miss allusions to events and experiences referred to cryptically or jokingly – 'Remember when Jack wanted to swim the channel?' meaning he had accidentally fallen in when paddling. They miss shared hidden meanings and find metaphors such as 'he's a pussycat' and idioms like 'it's raining cats and dogs' very puzzling. By responding literally they may unwittingly draw attention to themselves and are often found on the outside of groups.

An adult with ASD was reflecting on his experiences and spoke of his confusion trying to understand what was really meant at times. He worked out that if someone said something confusing with a smile it was a joke – this meant someone was pleased and that he was expected to smile too. If it was said without a smile it was meant unkindly and was sarcastic – this meant someone was displeased about something he had said or done, but he didn't know why or what should be changed.

Pupils with ASD become better at understanding non-literal language as they grow older but do not become skilled. They usually need more time to work out what is required and then do it. As this is a time-consuming process, the pupil may miss the next piece of information, a possible vital link in a sequence or step in an argument or instruction.

Strategies

- Keep language simple, direct and unambiguous. Explain idioms as they arise.
- Teach common idioms such as 'full of beans'.
- Allow processing time between 'bits' of information.
- Make references explicit – to last week, to earlier work, to the knowledge on which he is expected to build. Use visual cues to supplement language.
- Give a synopsis of what is coming, i.e. the subject, setting and time. Provide names in advance: 'Michael, this is a true account of what happened to a girl called Anne who lived in Holland at the time of the Second World War ...'
- Help him prioritise – 'The most important thing to remember is ...' – as he may get bogged down by detail.
- Use 'signposts' before and during verbal instruction: 'First of all ... and the second thing ... then ... finally ... to sum up ...'
  Use visual prompts and reminders if possible.
- Be clear about goals and expectations and what the child will be expected to do/know at the end.
- Explain to the child how he will know he has finished the task satisfactorily and then what he should do.
- Teach metaphors. Start with attribution (the qualities and properties of things, such as red, sweet, cold etc). Show how one thing can be likened to another as in similes, such as 'the sky was like lead'. Explain how attaching the attribute of something else makes a metaphor, as in 'the sky was leaden', but that this is not literally true.

Comprehension 2

Inference

When pupils are expected to make inferences they are being asked to perform sophisticated operations which can be difficult for many of them. Inference is regarded as a higher order comprehension skill that develops with maturity and practice. It involves being able to recognise meaning referred to indirectly.

In order to infer, a person has to know how to:

- imply or express something indirectly;
- insinuate, hint, give meaning through suggestion;
- deduce from what has gone before;
- understand consequences;
- draw a conclusion from something suggested or proposed.

A pupil with ASD is not likely to do any of these things when speaking or writing, still less recognise when others are making inferences. He does not understand or recognise hints and suggestions – he may well not understand that he is required to do something with information he has been given. He needs help to recognise that there is/may be a hidden meaning in what he hears or reads and needs assistance to develop his awareness and skills and to make links.

He may understand cause and effect and consequences when he does not have to process other information at the same time, such as remember names or new vocabulary. Other factors such as where he is, how comfortable he is with other people and their proximity, anxiety, distractions etc. all affect his ability to make sense of what he sees, is told or reads.

Much of social communication is also indirect. Actions and words which relate to people, their thoughts, feelings and behaviour may be obscure and of little interest, although they are the very stuff of soap operas, drama and fiction.

Strategies

- Be direct and explicit. Explain/teach how things, people and states of mind can be referred to indirectly. Give him practice at changing direct statements into indirect ones.
- Use drama and role play to help him to understand indirect language. The pupil can play different roles to allow him to understand the same situation from another person's point of view.
- Use pictures to encourage inference and storymaking.
- Use written language and texts to show the cues which give rise to inferential understanding because it is not ephemeral.
- Don't assume he understands – check and be explicit about the steps needed to move from one understanding to another.
- Ideas for teaching inference and higher order comprehension skills can be found in English course books and in thinking skills books (see Section 4, Resources).
- Use photos to teach cause and effect and the consequences of his actions.
- Use non-verbal activities to increase his awareness of gesture, tone and facial expression in order to aid his understanding of spoken communication.

Comprehension 3

Verbal reasoning

Children with ASD may be slower than others building up abstract concepts. Sometimes the difficulty may be in specific areas, for example space and time. The pattern of strengths and weaknesses may change over time as pupils develop the ability to reason from spoken and written language.

Some older children may be poor at making analogies, which involves seeing how things are alike; or in making opposite analogies which involves seeing differences. There are children who find it hard to make predictions because they do not know what to take into consideration. They may not know what is relevant. They may not have a shared understanding of cause and effect.

Some children cannot understand verbal absurdities, which often involve inference. For instance (depending on age) they may not initially see what is absurd about the old children's rhyme, 'One fine day in the middle of the night, Two dead men got up to fight ...', or understand the story about the boy who put bicycle patches on his tyres so the next time they were punctured they were already mended.

They find it hard to recognise incongruity because of their lack of life experience and ability to supply different contexts in which to understand what is said. They tend to learn much less incidentally than other children. For instance, they may not understand the real meaning of the story about the soldier's mother who said that everyone else in his company was out of step but her son. To properly understand this, another context is necessary, which includes knowledge of military drill and goes beyond the mother's perceptions. People with ASD find it hard to supply different contexts to see if there is another way of understanding, and become used to sticking with the first conclusion or remaining in a state of confusion. For them, understanding is a psycholinguistic guessing game.

These are difficult areas, especially as you may not know if the pupil's understanding entirely corresponds to your own.

Strategies

- Use the advice given for literal understanding regarding teaching attributes and similes as this is necessary for making analogies.
- Be direct in your own spoken language and explain all non-literal language. Highlight connections between ideas where possible.
- See Section 4 for resources that contain activities to develop higher order comprehension skills.
- Recognise this difficulty as a characteristic of ASD which should improve with help but which will not go away, so be realistic in your expectations of a particular child, accepting that most of the time he will be doing his best to understand.

Comprehension 4

Following instructions

Some children with ASD do not follow instructions even when you think they must have understood, perhaps because they do not realise the instruction refers to them if it is addressed to the whole class.

The child may not pick up on what others are doing because he has little interest in watching or imitating others in order to follow instructions. There may be other distractions in the room, such as sound or movement, that will occupy him and he may not give the instruction adequate attention. Sometimes the child has his own fixed idea about how something should be done and this prevents him from following your instruction.

His own interests and obsessions may also prevent him from hearing and dealing with words not connected with these. He may not be motivated in the same way as his peers because he lacks any desire to please his teachers.

Strategies

- Keep language simple and to the point.
- If possible, say what **is** to be done rather than what is **not** to be done.
- Don't expand instructions or add redundant information.
- Preface the instruction with the child's name and make sure you have his attention before you start.
- When giving instructions, do it at a time when there are no distractions such as other children moving about, noise from another classroom, grass cutting etc.
- Check the child's understanding by asking him to tell you, or another child, what he has been told to do.
- Reinforce your verbal message with visual support such as a symbol, picture or sequence of pictures. For instance, cards to illustrate wearing a coat and where to play could be held up to reinforce the instruction, 'Put on your coat and go out to play. Play on the yard and not on the grass.'
- Give instructions in small 'chunks', with time in between to allow the child to process information. This is especially necessary for children who have memory difficulties and find it hard to remember sequences.
- Use a social story to describe and reinforce desired behaviour (see Section 2).
- Use a reward system to reinforce desired behaviour.

Suggestions for IEP targets

These should be Specific, Measurable, Achievable, Relevant, Timed (i.e. **SMART**).

Inevitably targets are going to be very specific for each child – it is not possible to make them universally relevant. Here are some which may prove helpful as a guide.

Desired behaviour For (*name of child*) to:	**Suggested strategy** (specify reward system)
understand *attribution/ similes/metaphors*	use (*name book, resources chosen*)
understand idioms and expressions	
say when he is confused by *putting up his hand/asking LSA/teacher* at appropriate moment	decide what child is to do, when and where practise
recognise a *suggestion/hint/ consequence*	teach and practise
make simple inferences in *English/science/ humanities*	prepare questions about topic beforehand to provoke inference
draw conclusions from his reading in *English/science/humanities*	prepare questions about topic beforehand to provoke him into drawing conclusions
follow class instructions straight away	social story reward system make a list of commonly used expressions at home and at school by relevant members of staff

Chapter 6: Social skills

Social context 1

Home/school relationships

Children with ASD do not readily make links between pieces of information. They may also make responses in one situation which they do not think applies to another, a typical example being the distinction they make between home and school. Some children do not want information to be shared between home and school. In particular, they may resent homework because in their view it is school-related and therefore intrudes into time set aside for their chosen leisure activities.

One of the core difficulties with ASD is 'central coherence deficit'. 'Central coherence' is thought to be the brain's processes of organisation, planning, working independently, recalling and building on ideas – all skills children will require to successfully manage homework. For some ASD children, set homework will be beyond their capabilities.

Meeting the social as well as academic demands of school can be exhausting and children will need time for individual activities that are comforting and rewarding to them. Because many pupils with ASD experience greater degrees of anxiety and distress than most other children, the desire to do what they want or need is compulsive; it is often a means of relieving stress.

Both parents and teachers will benefit from gaining an insight into the other part of the child's life, even if he does not understand the advantages. Using their unique knowledge of their child and his development, parents may have devised strategies that teachers could usefully employ in the school environment. Good home/school liaison will provide a consistency of approach and expectations, both of which have been shown to benefit children with ASD.

Strategies

- Ensure frequent and positive home/school liaison so all those involved with the child have an awareness of what is happening in his life. See Section 2 (Home/school liaison) for ideas to facilitate communication between home and school.
- Examine the school's homework policy and consider what is useful and relevant in the light of the child's total needs.
- Determine how much homework could be accommodated at school (e.g. through a homework club).
- Consider negotiating a homework contract. This should involve and be supported by parents as they will be responsible for supervising the child.

Social context 2

Social cues

As already stated, people with ASD are not sensitive to social cues – they do not readily recognise the non-verbal signals used to convey feelings and states of mind. This is one of the reasons why they may talk for too long about their own interests and are not aware that they may be, and often are, boring to other listeners.

They are also often unaware of the correct way to approach people in different situations. Children with ASD may be over-familiar with adults, unable to recognise the subtle distinctions we make in our approaches to people of different status, age and occupation, dependent on particular situations. For instance the child in school may speak inappropriately to the chairman of the governors by addressing him as if he were his father; a stranger may be treated like a family friend. He needs to learn that different approaches and styles of speaking are required, depending on:

- his location (such as in church, at the shops, at a youth club, in the playground, in class);
- to whom he is talking (such as another pupil, a teacher, a policeman, a neighbour or relative);
- timing (such as at bedtime, during his family's favourite TV programme, when his mother is on the phone, during a school performance, when a discussion has reached its natural end).

He will not be sensitive to the social cues which would tell another child that his behaviour, language or timing is inappropriate in that context. He may also use inappropriate volume and his speech may be monotonous and lacking in intonation.

Strategies

- Use the social filing cabinet in Section 2 to teach the child about social contexts.
- Teach the child how to recognise the signs that people use to convey how they are feeling. Use a clip from a soap opera or film and analyse it for verbal cues such as sarcasm, humour and inference.
- The child must understand that cues may be non-verbal as well as verbal. Use a mute clip from a soap opera or film and analyse it for non-verbal cues.
- Use games and suggestions from Section 2 (Activities to promote non-verbal awareness).
- Help the child to become aware of:
  - **who** he can speak to about **what**
  - **how** he should speak and **when**.
- Analyse situations in which his problems recognising social cues have been an issue. Use role play and drama to demonstrate how he could have dealt with it differently.
- Use circle of friends (see Section 2) to teach appropriate responses depending on the position of different people in the circle.

Social context 3

Inappropriate behaviour

Children with ASD are usually oblivious to their inappropriate behaviour because they do not share the perceptions of others, one example being the 12-year-old girl who liked to pull her skirt up and could not see why this should be inappropriate at her age when it was tolerated in a younger child. This difficulty was solved by keeping her in trousers. Another boy picked his nose – he had no problem accepting someone else doing it so could not understand why others should object when he did it.

There are many behaviours which are offensive if carried out in the wrong context. Children with ASD need to be told clearly if their actions are likely to offend someone, what not to do and why. They may not understand the reasons and perhaps even enjoy others' responses to their actions, such as other children saying 'yuk!' pulling faces or laughing. A child may gain some satisfaction from a statement from an adult such as 'We don't do that, Stephen' when he just has! He may even decide others like him because of their response. It is probably impossible to try to stop behaviour such as masturbation or nose-picking – it is more realistic to say where and when it is permissible (e.g. when they are alone) and to encourage less offensive behaviour.

Much inappropriate behaviour can be accepted by others as merely eccentric, indicative of each person's uniqueness. This understanding should be fostered in school as a vital tool to prevent bullying.

Strategies

- Identify and teach the child to understand inappropriate behaviour and make suggestions for more acceptable types of behaviour.
- Use a social story to identify unacceptable behaviour and define clearly more desirable behaviour.
- The behaviour may be fulfilling a particular need in the child – if this is the case try to find an alternative way of meeting this need.
- Avoid an emotional response and give feedback in a neutral tone.
- Use the social filing cabinet in Section 2.
- Use assemblies and PSHE lessons to foster the inclusion of all and to celebrate the differences.
- If it is deemed necessary and appropriate, other children can be made aware of the child's difficulties and differences providing parental permission has been given. The agreement of the older child may also need to be sought.
- Other ideas for changing behaviour can be found in Chapter 1.

Social interaction 1

Making friends

Friendships involve interaction and shared interests. This is very difficult for young children with ASD because they may not be good at listening, watching and pausing to allow others to speak. They may not have a strong desire to communicate and may not be very interested in what others have to say. They find it hard to learn how to give and take turns. If the child does not do this naturally he is likely to have little empathy with others.

Almost all children by the age of six have developed a 'theory of mind' – they become aware that others have different knowledge and interests to their own. Development of this ability in children with ASD is much slower (often up to five years behind). It is easy to understand how a child without a fully developed 'theory of mind' is likely to impose his way of seeing things on others because he cannot comprehend that other ways are also valid. He is likely to find it hard to make and keep friends.

For some children, time spent on their own is important – it is not kind (or possible) to insist that they should become more social. However, a child with ASD must be given the opportunity to learn how to interact and make friends to allow him to join in should he want to be involved.

Strategies

- Teach the child the names of other children in his class.
- Encourage turntaking games, perhaps through circle time.
- Teach basic greetings by example and role play.
- Encourage the child to carry a toy or game which might arouse other children's interests and provoke friendly approaches.
- Encourage the understanding of non-verbal cues (see Section 2).
- Provide a 'playtime pal' for outdoor activities. The chosen 'pal' should encourage and play a favourite game/activity with the child (see also Ch. 1 and Section 2).
- Use a social story to help teach a specific strategy or reduce the incidence of a particular behaviour which is inhibiting or preventing social interaction.
- Allow the child to take 'time out' to be alone.

Social interaction 2

Keeping and sharing friends

Many children with ASD do develop friendships based on shared interests. In some cases there may be some form of reciprocal emotional support, often from children they have known all their lives and with whom they have grown up. In the main, however, they are friendships based on a coincidental interest or obsession.

Occasionally a young child with ASD may form a close attachment to another child and become upset if his friend plays with other children – because of his difficulty seeing things from another point of view he cannot understand how his friend can also be a friend to others. He may not know how to share toys – let alone time and space with other children – and may only be able to relate to his 'chosen' friend. Other children simply do not seem to have a real and separate existence for him.

Maintaining a friendship involves negotiation, a skill many children with ASD have difficulty acquiring (see 'theory of mind' above). Some older pupils are concerned at their lack of friends and aware that they are not popular, commonly being the last chosen for pairs and group work. They may want friends but at the same time do not have the skills necessary to be a friend and maintain a friendship. They may be aware they are missing something but not understand quite what. Some adolescents become depressed because of a lowering of their self-esteem.

The child with ASD may be socially isolated because he does not fit in with the others. Sometimes he may choose social isolation and will therefore appear to be aloof, not identifying with the group or sharing popular interests. Others in the class may well perceive this behaviour as judgemental, arrogant or odd, making it harder for the child to make friends. These children are extremely vulnerable to manipulation or bullying.

Strategies

- Brainstorm (in a group) 'What is a friend?' Use the points to discuss how to maintain friendships.
- Make a mindmap of 'What is a friend?' so it can be read again later and used as the basis for individual discussion or as the basis for a social story.
- Talk through some social stories about friendship.
- Encourage turntaking, perhaps through circle time.
- Use a 'buddy' system to involve other children.
- Use appropriate suggestions from Section 2 (Activities to promote non-verbal awareness).
- Use all opportunities to encourage a class identity of inclusion and caring which promotes understanding and collective responsibility for being friendly towards the child with ASD.
- Emphasise the child's strengths and interests to the class, and, if possible, encourage him to help others.
- Try to develop situations which promote social interaction.

Social interaction 3

Interactive play

Adults listen to their babies and naturally imitate the sound they make. They also 'speak' for them and reply as if the baby had communicated and made a comment or request. This leads to the baby copying the parents and is the beginning of eye contact, taking turns to 'speak' even before any words are known, i.e. non-verbal communication.

Many children with ASD do not respond in this way from the beginning although some parents report that their children seemed to be developing normally but stopped some time in their second year. At this age children with ASD are often given hearing assessments as they appear to be unable to hear.

One characteristic of ASD is the difficulty in developing understanding of non-verbal communication in addition to any problems in the development of the understanding of language. Because of this and other difficulties (e.g. social timing), children with ASD do not find verbal and social interaction enjoyable – they are often not interested in others and what they are doing, usually preferring to be on their own. As a consequence, these children are not learning with and from others.

A child who acts on and to his own agenda also lacks the skills of looking and listening; he is less likely to be able to interact successfully with others. As stated above, these communication difficulties affect the child's ability to relate appropriately to others and to make and keep friends.

Strategies

- Comment on what the young child is doing in his spontaneous play and time it to coincide with his actions. This will help him to learn that language corresponds to actions and is relevant.
- Join in and copy what the child is doing in his play. This has been shown to encourage the child to look at the adult's face more frequently and for longer periods.
- Play games with young children which include building up excitement through pauses, repetition and variation of volume.
- Play action songs with the child.
- Encourage turntaking, perhaps through circle time activities.
- Play games to encourage eye contact, awareness of facial expressions and body language (see non-verbal cues in Section 2).

Social interaction 4

Empathy and emotional understanding

A typical characteristic of ASD is the difficulty in acquiring a fully developed 'theory of mind' (see above). If you have acquired a 'theory of mind' you have some understanding of how others feel and think. Without it, there is only one way of seeing the world – your way. A consequence of this is the inability of the child with ASD to know what someone else is thinking and feeling. He lacks empathy. He does not have the ability to assume another person's personality, to imaginatively experience his experiences. His general lack of flexibility in his thinking and poor imaginative skills prevent him from connecting with other children to the extent that he can imagine their individual feelings.

Children with ASD are often perceived as cruel or cold – they can seem detached when others are physically or emotionally hurt, may laugh inappropriately and say and do things which appear malicious. These children do have ordinary human needs and feelings of their own but one reason they do not easily recognise them in others is that they do not easily recognise them in themselves. They can have real difficulty distinguishing one emotion from another, such as feeling upset from being cross, particularly when feelings overlap or are mixed. They find it hard to name the feeling and then verbalise what it is about. This limited recognition and insight into their own feelings interferes with their ability to understand the feelings of other children.

Human emotions can be frightening and confusing to a child with ASD – he may not know how to respond when someone requires emotional support (see Section 3). Allowances need to be made and his apparent coldness understood in the light of his understanding and ability.

Strategies

- Talk about emotions, name them, describe how they feel and their effect on the body. Role play different emotions to show their visual expression.
- Teach the child how emotions are often expressed non-verbally, e.g. tone of voice, body language and facial expression. Play games to promote awareness of non-verbal cues (see Section 2).
- Use stories to promote recognition and understanding of feelings and discuss responses to observed situations.
- Encourage the child to speculate on how others feel (in life and in fiction) and what response the other person may be expecting. Keep asking the child to relate this to his own experience and say how he would feel.
- Use a social story to teach a desired response to a specific situation.

Understanding others 1

Lies and other language uses

Most children – from quite a young age – tell lies to evade the consequences of an action. In the case of a simple lie, not much more than the awareness of cause and effect and some experience of the consequences is necessary for most children.

Some children with ASD do not lie and are perplexed and unsympathetic to other children's lies. If they do develop the ability to lie it is often at a later stage than others. The child with ASD may understand that by lying he can possibly avoid unpleasant consequences but he may not be a particularly good liar as this involves being imaginatively aware of what he needs to say so that someone else believes him. In contrast, there are some bright older children with ASD who learn to lie quite proficiently in order get something they want. However, their social naivety eventually catches them out as they cannot sustain the deception when the situation becomes more complex and it becomes obvious that they are lying.

Because children with ASD tend to have a black and white view of lying, and know it is wrong, they often have difficulty understanding why someone might use a white lie. A white lie also demands some awareness of how what is said can affect another's feelings. Most of these children would not use a white lie, irony, sarcasm, persuasion or double bluff because these involve manipulating the thinking of others. Therefore they are also largely unaware when others do this to them – even when they know someone is not speaking the truth they are still unlikely to understand the intention towards themselves.

Strategies

- Use real and fictional situations. Ask, 'Is that true? Why did he say it?' Explain the purpose of what is said if the child does not understand.
- Use drama to illustrate a situation in which someone reacts to being told:
  - the truth and a lie;
  - the truth and a white lie;
  - the truth, a lie, and a double bluff.

If appropriate appoint the child as the director of the scene. He should tell the other actors how to respond.

- Teach about language purposes and intentions as appropriate for that child, i.e. to deceive (lie, white lie), to avoid hurting someone's feelings (white lie), to manipulate someone (persuasion), to sneer and make someone feel bad about themselves (sarcasm).
- Discuss with the older child the potential and real consequences of lying once he is capable of understanding the moral issues. It is important to understand why a child may lie and if there is any intent to hurt another child for reasons which would be spurious to others. This is probably best done by a mentor.

Understanding others 2

Jokes

Slapstick humour is readily understood by all. However, verbal humour requires a degree of knowledge about what others know and expect to happen. This makes it more difficult for children with ASD to tell and appreciate jokes.

Verbal jokes work when both parties have an understanding of what is congruous and incongruous. They share an understanding of what is predictable and can appreciate when an unexpected response is made. The child with ASD desires predictability. He likes to have control over events in his life and is unlikely to be amused by the unpredictable, which usually makes him anxious and confused. Verbal humour often leaves the child with ASD perplexed, unfortunately setting him apart from others because he can't share their jokes. His own attempts to make jokes may appear ponderous and unfunny. Even funny jokes lose their humour if explained so if the child with ASD does not understand at first he is unlikely to find it funny even when it is explained.

The child with ASD will also find it difficult to appreciate class tricks played on another child or the teacher which are done 'for a joke', and is likely to want to 'tell tales', creating a social difficulty for himself.

Strategies

- Teach the child that smiling and laughter are expressions of amusement. Explain that jokes are things which are done or said to make someone laugh. Encourage him to notice and record what makes others laugh and what makes him amused, entertained and diverted.
- Use examples from class to explain how jokes usually involve saying something unexpected and that it is the incongruous and unexpected idea or image which makes people laugh.
- Tell him that there are different types of jokes – 'Knock knock' and 'Doctor, doctor' etc. Teach the child how they work. Let him look at age-appropriate joke books and talk about what he understands and likes.
- Encourage him to learn to tell a selected joke.
- Explain to him and to the class that humour is individual and it is OK not to laugh.
- Try to ensure the other children in the class do not make jokes at his expense or allow him to feel isolated because he cannot share the joke.

Understanding others 3

Accidents and bullying

An accident is an unplanned event which usually happens by chance. Most children with ASD will understand this if it is they who do something unintentional and cause an accident. They are often quite emphatic that it is not their fault.

However, they are much less likely to recognise that something that causes them stress and annoyance may also be accidental. They tend to perceive the effect of the incident – being bumped into, accidentally hit – as intentional and deliberate. In their view it happened, therefore someone meant to do it. As a result, retaliation may well follow and what was a minor incident can escalate into a major event.

This misperception arises out of the child's difficulty in mind reading and understanding others' intentions and states of mind (see Ch. 2, Seeing the bigger picture) – the bits that are missing are those they don't or can't perceive. Children with ASD may also perceive accidents as deliberate bullying and respond accordingly. They often have difficulties interpreting the difference between normal childhood banter and bullying and may complain to staff and carers – some adult reprimands may even be regarded by the child as bullying.

A child with ASD is unlikely to indulge in deliberate bullying but he may sometimes upset others by reacting angrily to a particular situation or by trying to impose his control over them.

Strategies

- Teach the child the difference between a planned and unplanned event. Use drama and role play to act out a likely incident. The children could play different roles in the same incident. The child with ASD can then at least see the event from an observer's point of view, or join in and play one of the parts so that he can experience different ways of understanding the same event.

- Talk about chance, fault, blame and responsibility and encourage him to use the words appropriately. Relate these words to class activities including video and stories.

- Make sure the child is not in fact being bullied. Follow the school's procedures if this is an issue.

- Provide a mentor to whom the child can go to discuss incidents he finds perplexing and distressing. This mentor needs to:
  - listen to him;
  - help him shift perceptions through discussion;
  - help him develop more appropriate and constructive strategies to cope with similar incidents;
  - encourage him to be positive about his successes.

- Ensure open and friendly liaison with home so that parents are aware of the full facts, not just their child's version of events.

- Make the child aware of any aspects of his behaviour to others that may be causing some distress and which could be changed.

- Use a social story to help change any specific behaviour or misunderstanding.

Suggestions for IEP targets

These should be Specific, Measurable, Achievable, Relevant, Timed (i.e. **SMART**).

Inevitably targets are going to be very specific for each child – it is not possible to make them universally relevant. Here are some which may prove helpful as a guide.

Desired behaviour For (*name of child*) to:	Suggested strategy (specify reward system)
carry out appropriate and satisfactory amounts of homework	liaise with parents review homework policy homework contract homework club social story
carry liaison book between home and school	social story agreed reminders at home and school
reduce inappropriate behaviour (*specify*)	social story social filing cabinet
develop awareness of social cues (*specify*)	circle of friends social story social filing cabinet
approach/respond to others appropriately	teach basic greetings and responses carry an interesting toy/object
join in activities appropriately by (*specify*)	social story buddy system circle of friends
recognise a *lie/white lie/persuasion/joke* and understand the reason for them	social story role play and drama talk about real and imaginary situations
accept that something is an accident	mentoring social story role play and drama
follow (*specify procedures*) when he feels he has been bullied	social story role play and drama

General strategies

1. Social stories

Social stories were devised by Carol Gray to use with children on the autistic spectrum.

Why use social stories?

- A social story is a short story written in a specific style and format. Each social story describes a situation or skill. It states a desired outcome and tells the child what he should do.
- The goal is to describe the situation and possible responses rather than to direct the child.
- Social stories eliminate the need to understand gestures, body language, words, intonation etc. – they give the child direct factual information.
- **Only one social story should be used at any time.**

Preparing a social story

- Choose just one behaviour to target within the social story.
- Identify the situation which causes most concern.
- Talk to any involved adults to find out the exact nature of the difficulty.
- Create the story using photographs, pictures or words according to the child's level of understanding, e.g. one page of writing or a mini photo album. The photos could illustrate the expected behaviour, for example lining up properly. An ICT program such as Inclusive Writer could be used for illustrations.
- Be positive and avoid using the phrase 'do not'.
- Avoid terms such as 'always', 'instead', and use terms such as 'usually' or 'sometimes' when describing the situation.
- The last directive sentence should start 'I will try' rather than 'I must' or 'I will'.

Introducing the story

- Choose a quiet place.
- Read before the target situation as often as necessary.
- Read it exactly as written.
- Give the story to the child in a format of his choice (e.g. in a book, on coloured paper, a laminated sheet etc.).
- Emphasise the child's ownership of the story.

And then ...

- Monitor the situation closely.
- When the story has proved successful, reduce the reading after discussion with the appropriate professional.
- If the story needs modifying, contact the appropriate professional.

Social Stories
Listening to Mrs Smith

Most Fridays Class 4 go to the hall for assembly. The children sit on the floor. We usually sing a song and listen to Mrs Smith.

Mrs Smith likes all the children to listen when she is speaking. Mrs Smith does not like anyone to interrupt when she is speaking.

I can help Mrs Smith by listening to what she says.

Social Stories
Stopping my work

Every day in class Mrs Brown asks the children to stop working. When Mrs Brown says **'STOP'** all the children stop and listen.

Stopping when asked is very important. This will make Mrs Brown very happy.

I will try to remember to stop my work as soon as Mrs Brown says **'STOP'**.

SOCIAL STORIES
BILLY'S STORY

A fire extinguisher is red and black.
Fire extinguishers are in the shops.

Fire extinguishers put out fires. They will
not hurt me.

I will try and hold Mum's hand and walk
past the fire extinguisher in the shop.

2. Circle of friends

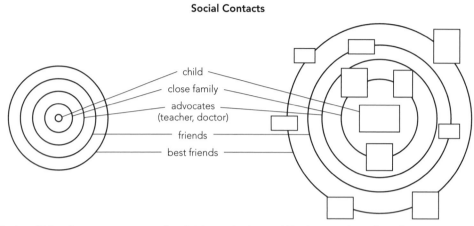

Social Contacts

Circle of friends is a programme for children who have difficulties making friends.

It is a map of a child's social contacts. It shows the support available from the immediate family, the advocates of the child, then friends and best friends.

A child with social difficulties may well have no one in the outside ring and perhaps only one or two, if that, in the 'friends' rings.

Mapping a child's circle of friends can be helpful. The map can be shared with the class by drawing it on the board and photos and pictures attached.

Children are asked to volunteer to be in the child's circle. They will greet the child, be friendly and helpful and act as mentors or 'buddies'.

A meeting can be held once a week to decide what was good or difficult about being a friend, what went wrong, and how to make changes next week to improve things.

The goal is to create a situation in which everyone learns and friendship develops.

Figure 2.1 Circle of friends 1

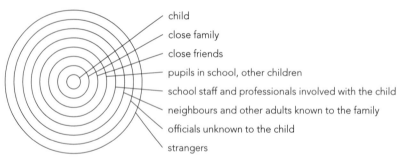

The circle of friends map can be used to show levels of contact, from intimate to increasingly distant.

Relating contacts to levels can help in the teaching of appropriate relationships.

Draw the map and use photos and pictures to help the child see and relate to the different levels of relationship. Drama and role play will also help the child learn who and how to approach in a more vivid way.

Use the levels of contact map to teach the child about:

- **greetings**. (Teach that hugs and kisses are appropriate to the level of friends, but not to other pupils, school staff, policemen and strangers.)
- **asking permission**. (Teach 'put your hand up in class at school and wait'.)
- **asking for clarification**. (Teach 'put your hand up at school'. Say 'Excuse me, I didn't understand.' to other outer levels.)
- **attracting attention**. (Teach how to say 'Excuse me' and 'Please', where *not* to shout out, tap someone, who *not* to start conversations with.)
- **asking for help**. (Teach how to approach and who it is safe to approach at different levels and in different settings.)

Figure 2.2 Circle of friends 2

3. Using a buddy system

This is a means of helping a child with a particular difficulty by enlisting the help of another, who becomes the child's **buddy**.

The help must be specifically directed, and both buddy and child clear about what is to be done, when and where, and by whom. Here are just some of the tasks buddies have successfully undertaken:

- Checking the child's homework diary, making sure he has what is needed for homework.
- Checking instructions copied from the board, and if necessary, writing them for the child in the homework diary – useful for directions such as 'bring visit money in by Thursday', 'PE is on Thursday this week – bring PE kit', 'swimming on Friday' etc.
- Writing down similar instructions when they are given verbally to make sure the child does not forget.
- Escorting a child who takes longer to get to class by bringing him from the playground five minutes earlier so the child is in class at the correct time.
- Escorting a child when moving round the school to make sure he gets to the right place.
- Checking that the child has the equipment needed for each lesson.

The buddy must be acceptable to the child, perhaps even suggested by the child, and in his class.

The buddy needs to be socially responsible and fairly sensitive so that help is not heavy handed or inappropriate. Some training may need to be given as well as opportunities to review the situation at least weekly. The help should be given in a matter of fact, low-key way – perhaps more than one child in the class could have a buddy.

Buddies must not feel the task is a burden. They are not ultimately responsible for the child and help needs to be accepted willingly by the child. Being a buddy can be shared between children perhaps on a weekly basis and could attract merit points.

4. Playtime strategies

Other children can be used to help and support children with ASD at playtimes providing they are willing and suitable, and it is mutually beneficial.

A system of 'playtime pals' can be set up. These are special, helpful friends who are chosen to play with a child for five minutes each break or playtime. The time is short to allow the child with ASD to be alone and de-stress during playtime if necessary.

The playtime pal system can work like this:

- Suitable children are chosen from the class.
- Their names are put in a box and the child with ASD chooses one or two names from the box at the beginning of the day (these names are then removed).
- The chosen children play with the child with ASD for a short while during each playtime.
- The subject of play is likely to be the child's choice to start with, but gradually the playtime pal should be allowed to choose a game as well from a selection which is familiar to the children.
- The play may be based on learning a particular playground game being taught and promoted that week.
- The child with ASD works through all the names in the box. When everyone has had a turn for a day, all the names are put back in to start again.
- Do not include the names of children who would be unsympathetic, antagonistic or in any other way unsuitable.

Friendship squad

Another approach is the 'friendship squad', i.e. children who apply to help in the playground. They act as positive role models and demonstrate caring and friendship. One of their roles involves playing with isolated children; this works well if the school has developed a positive playtime and lunchtime policy and has well thought-out anti-bullying strategies and sanctions. Schemes like this can be adapted or modified to cope with the specific but different needs of children with ASD.

See *All Year Round: Exciting Ideas for Peaceful Playtimes* by Jenny Mosley and Georgia Thorp (Section 4, Resources).

5. TEACCH approach

TEACCH (Treatment and Education of Autistic and Communication Handicapped Children) is a structured approach first developed in the early 1970s at the University of North Carolina by Eric Schopler. It was the first state-wide comprehensive community-based programme. This approach is used in the classroom with children with ASD who need the security of predictable structure and routine to enable independence.

The TEACCH programme relies heavily on physical structure and the visual presentation of all material. For some children with ASD verbal explanations are not always effective, therefore, pictures or written instructions are used to provide information or classroom instructions.

The programme is also designed to teach routines. For children with ASD, routines provide a strategy for understanding and predicting the order of events around them, helping to reduce anxiety. Some children devise their own routines which may not be adaptable or acceptable. When designing a routine or timetable, care should be taken to build in flexibility as this reflects everyday life.

The programme is designed specifically for each child depending on individual needs. In spite of the common features of autism, all children with ASD find it very difficult to learn in a group situation because they do not observe each other or see themselves as part of a group.

Central components of the TEACCH programmes are:

- the work station;
- the work system;
- the daily schedule.

The **work station** is a physical structure with clear boundaries:

- a screened work table or an area defined by coloured tape;
- no distractions or clutter.

The **work system** shows the pupil:

- what work is to be done;
- how much is to be done;
- what happens when it is finished.

Always work left to right, top to bottom. Use two trays or boxes labelled (i) work to do (on the left) and (ii) finished work (on the right).

The **schedule** is a **VISUAL** representation of the timetable for each day or half day. It may use:

- objects;
- photos;
- pictures/symbols (e.g. Inclusive Writer/Widgit);
- words.

These are usually fixed using velcro and displayed in the work station. Always present information **visually**:

- make expectations clear;
- highlight important information.

6. Visual schedules and transition planners

Visual schedules

A visual schedule represents the timetable for each day or half day. It may use:

- objects;
- photos;
- pictures/symbols (e.g. Inclusive Writer/Widgit);
- words.

It needs to be displayed prominently at eye height so the child can see what he is supposed to be doing and what will happen throughout the course of the day. If he has a work station then it should be displayed on the wall facing the child. A velcro strip on the wall with velcro attached to the back of picture, photo or word cards is a useful way of keeping cards in place. At its most sophisticated the schedule becomes a weekly timetable, but at an early stage much smaller time periods are best shown.

In some cases the child may carry a duplicate card to remind him of the activity he has yet to complete. At the end of the activity this card can be returned to a tray, pocket or box for completed activities. The child needs to learn that the activity is not completed until the card is returned to its box.

The child needs to be talked through the day or half day. This is a good way of teaching and reinforcing time vocabulary with the use of words such as *now, then, next, later, after,* and spatial vocabulary such as *in the hall, at the painting table* etc.

Transition planners

These represent a variation on the visual schedule and are aimed at helping children maintain as high a level of independence as possible. The planner is placed at a fixed point such as the side of a cupboard or a noticeboard where it can be seen easily and passed frequently.

At first pictures can be attached to the planner (as in the visual schedule), showing what is happening that day, for how long and in what order. As the child gets older and becomes familiar with using the planner it can be produced in a portable format (such as a daily timetable sheet or diary) for the child to refer to at any point throughout the day. It can be placed on a desk or special place in each of the areas the child visits, or carried round in his bag. Its purpose is to help him through transitions, i.e. changing activities and rooms.

A teacher/mentor/LSA can check the events of the day with the child to make sure he knows about changes in teacher, classroom and routine so that there are no surprises.

7. Setting up a work station

Ideally this should consist of two tables:

- one for supported teaching when you teach the child and prepare him to work independently;
- the other for independent work.

If this is not possible, put cards on the table or wall to show the child for which purpose the station is being used. Put the table(s) against a plain wall or partition. Try to put screens or barriers at either side so that on three sides the child is not distracted. Do not decorate the area as the idea is to reduce distraction – just attach a daily schedule on the facing wall and perhaps a social story if one is being used.

On the independent work table place two labelled baskets or trays for

- **work to be done** positioned on the **left** of the child;
- **finished work** placed on the **right** of the child.

Setting up a daily schedule

- This can be set up on a board. Cards – which can be attached and moved around as needed – should show *all* the events of the day at first, including assembly, breaks and lunchtime. In time it is likely to become less detailed.
- The schedule should run left to right, top to bottom, as in reading. The cards can be attached showing the order of events for the day.
- The cards should have pictures, symbols, photographs or words which the child recognises and understands.
- The child should be involved in setting up and checking the schedule frequently. He may like to remove the cards as he moves through the day, or you can develop a way of ticking off each completed activity.

Older children could carry clipboards around with a task sheet to be ticked when tasks are successfully completed. If the lesson or activity can be broken down into smaller parts, the child can tick each of the completed parts. You could relate this to a reward system.

8. The social filing cabinet

Aims

This activity aims to help children understand how to predict, anticipate and act in different situations with different people. The child's family will need to provide names and perhaps photographs of family members, etc. It is important to note that this activity must be part of a total approach to help the child develop social skills and understanding. It is a deliberate attempt to make the child think about subtle social distinctions and how to deal with and respond appropriately to certain situations, a skill people without ASD develop naturally.

People files

Activity one: Building a social filing cabinet

In this activity you are building an individual file of the people within the child's own social circle. This could take time, so perhaps just start with family and close friends. However it is important for children to also learn about acceptable levels of familiarity with other adults.

1 Family

2 Close friends

3 Adults in school

4 Pupils in school – other children

5 People in authority

6 Neighbours and other adults

This could be done in a variety of ways according to the age, level of understanding and ability of the child. Some children prefer photographs, others could develop their own pictures using computer imaging. The cards could be displayed in a social filing cabinet or in pockets and then transferred into a book for the child to keep. It should be kept up to date with new entries.

Figure 2.3 An example of a social filing cabinet

Manners file

The following activities are designed to help the child develop his manners file. It is important for children to learn that there are unwritten social rules about how we behave towards others and how we speak to them.

Activity two: What to do and what not to do

Talk about kissing, touching and stroking. If appropriate, create some picture cards of these activities. Explain who it is appropriate to touch in this way, for example, he can stroke his dog and kiss and cuddle his mum but not his teacher. Match the activity to the 'people' files in the child's social filing cabinet.

Use the 'What *not* to do' cards to help the child learn that there are also things we never do to others, such as kick, bite, pinch, etc. These go into the rubbish bin.

Activity three: What to say

Put these on cards:

- Say hello and goodbye.
- Say you don't like something.
- Say you like something.
- Ask for something.
- Ask questions.
- Get someone to listen to you.
- Say it is not your fault.

Match these cards to the 'people' files and encourage the child to tell you what he would say to the people in his file. Discard unacceptable responses in the rubbish bin.

Activity four: Talking to different people

Family

Ask the child to draw a family tree if he can. Encourage him to think about the roles of different people, especially different generations. Talk about the difference in the way he speaks to his parents and grandparents, with questions such as:

- How would he say hello to his grandma?
- How would he say hello to his mum?
- What does he like to talk about with his granddad?
- What does he like to talk about with his dad?
- Ask him if he behaves and speaks in the same way to his mum *and* his dad if:
    he is tired
    he is hungry
    he is hurt
    he is upset.

Do they both treat him in the same way at these times?

- Ask him about his brother/sister/cousins.
- How does he ask them to help him tidy up for instance?
- What does he say to them if he is cross with them?
- How do they speak to him?

Friends

- Make a 'family tree' of friends. Group them according to interests or how he knows them, for example, a branch for those with whom he shares an interest, or those who are the children of his parents' friends.
- Write down some of the things he likes to do with his friends.
- What can he talk about to friends? Would he speak to them in the same way that he speaks to his grandma? What is different?
- Think about teasing. What sort of things do friends say to tease or joke? How can he react when this happens?
- Make a list of his friends and write opposite each one what they like and why he likes them.

In school

Draw a 'school' tree using these questions to help:

- Who is the leader in a school? What things does he have to do that is different from other teachers? How should the child speak to this person in school?
- What is the teacher's name? Why are teachers called Mr, Miss or Mrs? How are teachers greeted?

Figure 2.4 The rubbish bin

- Why should pupils put up their hand in class and not call out?
- What do caretakers and lunchtime supervisors do and how should they be addressed?

Figure 2.5 What *not* to do cards

9. Home/school liaison

Some schools liaise with parents through the use of a Dictaphone. When this is not possible (or desirable), other forms of communication need to be developed. The following prompt sheet and record sheets are useful to help parents and school understand what is happening to the child when he cannot/doesn't wish to say.

Choose the style best suited for the age and difficulties of the child, and send a page home each day, either tucked into a reading folder or glued into an exercise book. The completed record sheets can be kept in a polythene pocket. They are often a useful reference tool that can provide a pattern over time.

The 'today at school' page can act as a prompt sheet. An adult should help the child circle the activities and the parents can use the pictures as prompts to encourage talk. A spare sheet of pictures is included for cutting up and using in a different format, if desired. Similarly, the record sheets can act as prompts to encourage talk about what has happened and what is going to happen. An agreed code for behaviour can be used if desired (see Figs 2.6 and 2.7).

These sheets can help the child to:

- Understand what is and is not shared knowledge.
- Organise memories of his experiences.
- Use more mature sentence grammar to respond to questions with opportunities to follow adult modelling.
- Extend his language uses.
- Develop more mature turntaking and conversation skills.
- Benefit from a more consistent approach from parents and school.

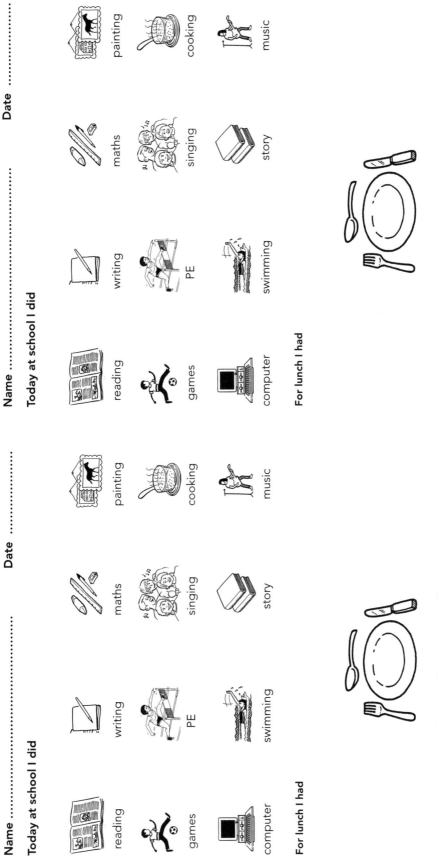

Figure 2.6 Prompt/record sheet – 'Today at school'

Name .... Date...............

Last night at home

For tea I ate ....
....

On TV I saw ....
....

I played ....
....

We went to ....
....

Our visitors were ....
....

I went to bed at ....
....

Name .... Date...............

Last night at home

For tea I ate ....
....

On TV I saw ....
....

I played ....
....

We went to ....
....

Our visitors were ....
....

I went to bed at ....
....

Figure 2.7 Prompt/record sheet – 'Last night at home'

School Record

Day: ....   Date: ....   Behaviour: 1 2 3 4 5

Lessons (a.m.)

Lunch/break

Lessons (p.m.)

Comments

Parent Record

Day: ....   Date: ....   Behaviour: 1 2 3 4 5

Tea

Evening

Bedtime

Getting up

Breakfast

Comments

School Record

Day: ....   Date: ....   Behaviour: 1 2 3 4 5

Lessons (a.m.)

Lunch/break

Lessons (p.m.)

Comments

Parent Record

Day: ....   Date: ....   Behaviour: 1 2 3 4 5

Tea

Evening

Bedtime

Getting up

Breakfast

Comments

Figure 2.8 School/parent record sheet

10. Conversation cue cards

- These can be glued to card and used as cue cards.

- They can act as the focus for discussion in a group (or one to one).

- They provide good prompts for role play. One or two people can model how *not* to stick to the rules, as well as what to do.

- They have been found to be particularly useful with older children. For instance, the card 'Working in a Group' has been used in small group situations, especially for group problem-solving activities in science. All children have to comply with the rules.

- Some children have benefited from the visual prompts, especially those who have not learned the unwritten rules of conversation.

LOOKING AT ANOTHER PERSON WHO IS SPEAKING

- helps you keep your mind on the same subject
- tells you how the person feels about what is being said

  You can tell how people feel by looking at:

- their faces and expressions
- their eyes
- their posture (how they sit, stand and move)

LOOKING AT ANOTHER PERSON WHILE YOU SPEAK

Tells you:

- if the person understands you
- if the person is interested in what you are saying
- how the person feels about what you are saying
- if you need to CHANGE anything so the person understands you better

  Things you might change:

- how fast you speak
- what tone you use
- how long you speak for. You will be able to see if the other person wants to ask you something or make a comment
- how much setting and context you need to give. If you haven't given enough the other person will be puzzled.

LISTENING TO ANOTHER PERSON'S VOICE TELLS YOU

- how the person feels about what he or she is saying
- how the person feels about the person being talked to

RULES OF GOOD LISTENING

1. look at the speaker
2. listen carefully
3. keep quiet
4. sit still

Figure 2.9 Conversation cue cards

TURNTAKING

means giving **everyone** who wants the chance to speak

– it means you must not talk too long

– you must stop after you have made one or two points

– you must give the other person a chance to respond

Conversation is like a ball

– it has to be thrown backwards and forwards

CONVERSATION means taking turns to speak

It means – listening to the other speakers

– one person speaks at a time

RULES OF CONVERSATION

1. sit still, don't fidget

2. look at the speaker

3. think about the words

4. don't butt in

IF YOU WANT TO JOIN IN

1. nod and agree with the speaker

2. stand by the person

3. wait for a pause

4. look at the person

5. ask a question or talk about the same thing

Figure 2.9 Conversation cue cards *Continued*

WORKING IN A GROUP

Rules

1. **NO ONE** is more important than another

2. **EVERYONE** should have something to do for part of the task

3. **BRAINSTORM** for ideas of what to do, how to do it, what order to do it in

A **BRAINSTORM** means **everyone** gives ideas

- all ideas are equally valid

- no criticism is allowed

If you CAN'T AGREE

- vote and accept the majority decision

- take turns to make decisions

CRITICISM IS GOOD when

- it is helpful

- it makes the other person feel better

- it is honest

- it doesn't hurt anyone's feelings

CRITICISM IS BAD when

- it is something which can't be changed like how someone looks, how clever someone is etc.

- it makes a person feel bad

- it is done in front of other people

- it is not clear so it is not helpful

- it doesn't tell you what to do to make things better

- it is not fair

- it is not honest

Figure 2.9 Conversation cue cards *Continued*

11. Organisation strategies

School can:

- ensure adequate and appropriate storage is available;
- minimise the amount of equipment and number of books needed;
- colour code subject books;
- maintain good links with home and exchange information.

Getting through the day

- establish timetable/routines for each day (send a copy home);
- provide an equipment list for each day (send a copy home);
- devise a checklist or ticklist of what is required for each lesson;
- ensure good use of homework or home/school diary.

Within and between lessons

- use visual support to help with the sequencing of tasks and organisation of activities such as a visual 'menu' or flowchart, or use strategies such as storylines. A storyline is a line used to express a period of time – events and activities can be represented by diagrams or words (in chronological order) and joined to the storyline to create a visual record. The line is usually drawn to run down the page from top left to bottom right. It can also be used as a planning tool for spoken and written language activities, and as a strategy to recall events in the order they happened such as a school trip, an assembly or an altercation in the playground;
- ask the child to report at specified intervals for checking, e.g. half a page, three sums, five minutes;
- help with timing/changing activities:
  - by warning of the imminent end of a lesson
  - allowing extra time to pack up and organise equipment to avoid panic and stress
  - use a timer or visual reminder.

Teachers can:

- have realistic expectations of the difficulty and duration of the task;
- be clear about what is required and when it is finished;
- allow time for information to be processed and check understanding by asking the child to report back;
- keep language simple and avoid the use of metaphors, idioms, non-literal language and indirect requests – if they must be used, check understanding and teach their meaning;
- give 'signposts' in their instructions, such as: You will need to know because ... firstly, ... next ... last/finally ... how long until ... ? how long since ... ?

Name ....   Date ....

TASK	DONE ✓

Figure 2.10 Task sheet

12. Suggestions to improve motor skills

Helping the child with poor gross motor skills

Learning new skills

These can be incorporated into a PE lesson and aimed at improving:

- **balancing** – Walk along lines, on benches, hopping, standing on one leg, step over canes, jump/hop into plastic hoops various distances apart, balance beanbags on various parts of the body. Play 'leaning tower' (forward, backwards, left, right) leaning without losing balance.
- **control of movement** – Move at different heights and speeds. Stop and start, rolling, moving and turning left and right.
- **muscle tone** – Stepping, cat springs, crouch jumps.
- **motor planning** – Obstacle races, zigzagging round skittles, climb ladders, steps.
- **movement memory** – 'Follow my leader', watch and copy movement sequences.
- **body image/awareness** – learn to name and recognise body parts. Play 'hot dog' game (roll child in blanket, touch and name part). Roll ball on different parts of body, ask child to identify part.
- **co-ordination** – throw paper/soft balls into a basket, varying distance. Roll, chase, catch balls. Dribble, kick balls, bat and ball skills. Throw/roll balls at targets.

Modifying the learning and physical environment

- Make sure the task is not too difficult or the steps too large.
- Learn to name body parts such as: wrist, finger, palm, knee, shoulder, ankle, toes; and movements such as: stretch, trace, circle, turn, twist, reach left, right, hop, skip, crouch, stoop. Then use this language to control movements.
- Use 'hedgehog' balls at first because they are easier to catch.
- Use 'scratch' balls and gloves with velcro pads.

Helping the child with fine motor skills

Learning new skills

- Play games with **pickup sticks**, matchsticks.
- Spin **coins**.
- Copy and create patterns on **pegboards**.
- **Thread beads** on coat hanger wire, string etc.
- Play **tiddlywinks**.
- **Construction toys**.
- **Cutting**.
- Use **clothes pegs** on the edges of paper, round cans, make peg trains.
- **Sand and water play** for pouring.

- Play **finger walking** – hands like spiders, travel across surfaces, use all fingers. Alternate hands, then simultaneously.
- **Finger rhymes**. Use poems and tapes. Aim to have a quick response with independent finger movements, plus curling fingers into the palm, stretching.
- **Finger puppets**. Palms up, spread hands then close again – together and separately. Also place palm down, lift up each finger independently.
- **Finger flicking**. Flick counter, cubes down a track. Throw dice to identify which finger to use (1–5 each finger, 6: change hands, then throw again for which finger to use).
- **Piano playing**. On varied surfaces and instruments, play 'scales' up and backwards.
- **Touch and move**. Both hands palm up on table. Adult touches one finger, child moves same finger on other hand. Try palms down, then adult touches the hand behind the child's back.
- **Thumb touching**. Touch each finger in turn with thumb, separate hands then both together.

Modifying the physical and learning environment

- **Cutting**
  - make sure scissors are correct (either for left or right hand) and sharp enough to cut;
  - use stiff paper before soft materials;
  - card can be stuck on the back of paper to act as a scissor guide;
  - grade tasks, e.g. cut a fringe, cut between two lines (reduce distance) follow a line, then curve left and right (learn cut-stop-change direction-cut), combine lines and turns, cut out simple shapes, cut round edge of picture.
- **Table and chair**. Chairs should be one-third of the child's height, the table half the child's height. A gently sloping surface (towards child) is best for drawing and writing.

Coping strategies

- ask an adult or other child to help;
- plan activity, practise skills, repeat instructions etc. beforehand.

Helping the child with poor dressing skills

Learning the skills

- Break down the task into steps for each item of clothing then teach one at a time, e.g. how to put socks/trousers on, tie shoelaces etc.
- Practise 'backward chaining', i.e. adult does whole sequence and child does the last bit. Gradually increase the last bit so the child has more and more to do.
- Practise 'backward chaining' for sequence of items for the child to put on/take off, e.g. adult dresses child except for last sock, then both socks, then jumper, sweatshirt etc. Decide a sequence and stick to it.

- When the child can put on all items of clothing, lay them out left to right in the order they have to be put on; child always follows the order; child can place clothes in right order.

Modifying the physical and learning environment

- use easy fastenings at first such as Velcro;
- clothes should not be too tight;
- no fiddly fastenings.

Strategies

- Make sure the child can name all items of clothing and their parts, knows left from right, up/down, top/bottom, over/under, front/back, inside/outside, upside down etc.
- Encourage body awareness through art, PE, touching games (name the body part), copying movements, copying games such as 'Simon says'.
- Don't rush the child – allow plenty of time.
- Reduce distractions so child can concentrate.
- Make a visual sequence to act as a prompt.

Helping the child with poor handwriting and drawing skills

Learning new skills

- teach numbers first (as there are fewer);
- teach correct number and letter formation from the start;
- teach letters in families;
- teach the child to write his/her name;
- encourage the dominant hand – pass things to that hand, hold pencil in it etc.;
- teach correct pencil grip right from the start, either tripod grip or, if that can't be maintained, the 'fiddle' finger hold (when the pencil/pen rests between the *fore* and *middle* fingers);
- teach the correct pressure (if too much pressure, put two pieces of carbon paper between three pieces of paper – the child should write without marking the bottom paper);
- do exercises to develop wrist, hand and finger strength (see fine motor skills);
- follow a writing/drawing programme;
- teach the left-handed procedure:
    - sit towards the right of the desk
    - put paper to the left of the body
    - rotate paper 32–45 degrees in a clockwise direction
    - support paper with the right hand
    - keep left writing forearm parallel to the paper
    - hold the pencil/pen so that the child can see what is being written and what has to be written.

Modifying the physical and learning environment

- use a pencil grip, such as Stetro, to help with holding pencil correctly;
- use ∆ shaped pens and pencils such as Berol 'handhuggers' for correct grip;
- use plain paper for learning letters, practising movement, controlling size, which is determined by arm and hand control;
- go on to lined paper from about six years old and continue to use appropriate-sized line guides for as long as needed;
- use 'handwriting' paper/books (with an extra line to indicate height of body of letters) as long as needed;
- use a vertical (upright) board so that 'up' and 'down' has meaning;
- if possible, use a sloping surface for writing – this particularly helps children with visual difficulties as well as other motor problems;
- the slope should be towards the child and the paper should be rotated to the same angle as the child's arm when writing;
- use appropriately-sized squared paper for sums to prevent column drift or use a template in the child's book;
- use a green-coloured dot to show where the child should start writing and a red dot indicating where to finish;
- use templates for different subjects, e.g. paper with lines for heading and date, boxes for pictures, guidelines for writing;
- the correct seating position is one-third of the height of the child, the table should be half the child's height;
- the child's bottom should be positioned at the back of the chair so the thighs are supported by the chair. Feet should be on the ground. Forearms should be supported by the table, and body and head should be upright not slumped.

Coping strategies

- an adult can 'scribe' for the child;
- use a Dictaphone;
- use ICT;
- use words on cards for assembly as in 'Breakthrough to Literacy';
- use storylines, diagrams and charts to support what is heard with visual representation;
- use a cartoon grid to record story/activity in order;
- use a task sheet to tick when the activity is completed (see Fig. 2.10).

Helping the child with visual processing and motor difficulties

Some children have visual motor difficulties which make it hard to track along a line or follow a moving object, particularly when it crosses the midline. This means that they cannot process effectively what they see and may be unable to locate an image quickly enough. They may find it difficult to judge speed, position in space, and the relation of one thing to another. They may also have figure/ground difficulties.

Visual processing difficulties often show as reading difficulties. The child with visual motor and/or processing difficulties may:

- have difficulty reading small print;
- have difficulty reading lines close together;
- miss lines out;
- reverse letters and/or words, such as was/saw;
- misread words, sometimes adding letters or deleting some;
- keep looking up or away;
- fix on distant objects;
- rub his eyes a lot;
- have 'teary' eyes which water, especially in bright light;
- shake his head or develop a tic;
- screw up his eyes;
- cover one eye;
- sit in an asymmetrical position;
- use avoidance strategies to get out of reading.

This means that in reading, he is likely to:

- see words or print moving though he may not say so;
- have difficulty focusing and refocusing on words moving along the line;
- have difficulty seeing letter sequences in the right order;
- have difficulty remembering sequences of letters;
- suffer from headaches in the frontal lobes.

When word, print and patterns are uncomfortable or even painful to look at this is called **pattern glare**. This can occur in reading when there is too great a contrast between print and paper, and when words and lines are too close together.

Some children are particularly susceptible to the flicker of fluorescent lights and computer screens. Flickering can cause frontal headaches and migraine, and can also affect hearing and balance.

Difficulties in class may be helped by:

- keeping classroom noise down;
- reducing visual distractions such as colours, patterns and movements;
- using a blue pen on a whiteboard, rather than red or yellow;
- using natural light in preference to artificial lights and replacing flickering bulbs as soon as possible.

Difficulties reading print will be helped if:

- there is reduced contrast between print and paper – use grey/black print on off white paper;
- print size is big;
- the print font is an old-fashioned round type;

- there are large spaces between words and good spaces between the lines;
- the margins around the print area are large;
- the print is not justified as this distorts letter size and spacing;
- lighting is good, preferably natural;
- a piece of card is used to aid the location of text on the page;
- texts are read on a sloping vertical surface;
- an adult reads aloud with the child, as in shared reading – this helps the child to build up eye movement control and stamina for reading.

If visual processing difficulties are suspected, the child should be referred to an optometrist for examination and advice. A letter of referral stating which difficulties have been observed in school will be helpful.

13. Activities to promote non-verbal awareness

Eye contact

Nose first The adult starts with touching her nose. Each child then has to copy the adult then add an action of his own. Each action should be different – try just face and head actions as well as whole body actions. Carry on until there are too many to remember.

Wink swap Pass the wink around the group (max. 8 pupils). Each child winks back at the child who winks at him, then winks at someone else, who passes it on ...

Catch the wink This can be varied by asking the children to start with closed eyes which they can open or close, but mustn't keep closed. Another child has to try to wink at the other children, catching them when their eyes are open. The winked-at children have to sit down until all have been winked at.

Wink murder (or wink sleep) Send a child out. Others decide which of them will be the murderer. When the murderer winks at a child, he will die. Bring in the detective, i.e. the child who was sent out. All the children keep looking at and making eye contact with each other. The murderer also keeps making eye contact with other children but does not have to wink every time. The detective has to try to intercept the wink and work out who is the murderer.

Look and offer Take in a packet of crisps (or similar). Each child has to offer the bag to another by looking him in the face and asking, 'Would you like a crisp?' The child responds by looking him in the eyes and saying, 'Yes please'. Take turns. This can be varied by offering a choice of crisps.

Pass the beanbag The children throw a beanbag to each other, but only to those who look directly at the thrower. The thrower then throws the beanbag to someone who makes eye contact with him.

Pass the ball The children stand in a circle facing inwards. One child stands in the middle. The other children pass a ball around the circle behind their backs. When he shouts 'freeze' the other children stop and the child in the middle has to try to guess where the ball is.

Sunglasses The teacher wears sunglasses or a mask, if the child is comfortable with this, to encourage focusing of attention to the upper face and eyes. Take turns.

Bubbles With little children, blow bubbles, catch with applicator and move in front of eyes so that the child may unintentionally make eye contact. This can be verbally reinforced with words such as 'Well done John, you could see my eyes when you looked at the bubble'.

Facial expressions

Feeling pairs Use pictures of faces showing emotions (for example, from Black Sheep Press, see Section 4, Resources). The child has to match picture cards showing the same emotions.

Velcro faces Use velcro pieces to create different expressions.

Copy faces The child has to copy the expression on a favourite character's face (such as Thomas the Tank Engine or the Simpsons). He can use a mirror to try to get a good match.

Mirrors In pairs, one child makes an expression and the other copies. Take turns and vary the expressions.

Face file Make a 'face file' book. Take photographs of people the child knows, e.g. parents, teachers, relatives and friends looking happy, sad, frightened, hurt, tired etc. Label each emotion and (with the child) under each picture list reasons why people might experience these emotions.

Tone of voice

Register voices The teacher names the emotion and the children in the class have to respond to the register saying their responses with appropriate emotion, such as happy/sad/cross. The emotion can be changed by the teacher at any time. Make sure there are a few pupils ahead of the child with ASD modelling correct responses until you are sure he can respond appropriately to the target emotion without notice.
This can be varied such as when reciting tables.
Many meanings Practise saying something in different tones of voice such as:
'Well done!' (as praise or criticism).
'He has shaved his head!' (as surprised, upset, amused).
'She has always liked spiders' (as disgusted, disbelieving, informatively).
'It's time to go' (with relief, as an order, bravely, nervously).
Word Stress (for older pupils) Say the same sentence putting the stress on a different word each time. Talk about the different message conveyed each time depending on how the words are stressed such as:
A few children say cheese smells disgusting.
Are you a happy person?
Is this object your coat?
I think she has a lovely voice.
Colourful voices Try linking tone of voice to colours to represent different feelings:
loud angry voice – red
loud happy voice – pink
loud frightened voice – purple
quiet sad voice – blue
quiet frightened voice – orange.
Let the child choose which colour best represents each tone of voice for him.

Body language

Silent movies Watch a mute TV soap, video or silent movie. Discuss what was going on and how you could tell.
Mirrors In pairs, one child does the actions and the other copies such as:

- domestic actions such as getting dressed, brushing teeth, eating, making a drink;
- work such as sweeping, sharpening pencils, washing windows, cutting grass;
- actions which demonstrate feelings, such as showing boredom (yawning, gazing around, time-filling activities, losing focus), impatience (tapping fingers, looking at watch), anticipation (excited walking, alert sitting, looking at watch), sadness (dejected walk, downward gaze, droopy body posture) etc.

Guess what To a group, the teacher models examples of body language and the children have to guess what is going on. The children then model their own examples of body language to the group. Situations to be modelled could include:

- looking for something on the floor – and finding it;
- lost keys in pocket;
- having a headache;
- having a sore tummy/leg/back etc.;
- crossing the road;
- feeling sad, happy, tired, cross etc.

Scenes Children act out particular situations, appropriate to their age, such as:

- sitting next to a stranger on a crowded bus;
- finding a seat in a crowded waiting room;
- asking someone in the street the time;
- asking someone for directions in a street, such as the post office, café etc;
- ordering food at a burger bar or in a café;
- getting to the checkout and finding that there isn't enough money to pay;
- discovering that a purse has been lost when the person is about to pay – on the bus, at a café, in the post office or shop;
- finding a purse/watch/valuables in the park, in a shop, on a bus, in the street.

14. The older pupil – a whole-school approach

A pupil with ASD cannot flourish, or maybe even cope at school particularly at Key Stages 3 and 4, without a whole-school policy committed to:

1 understanding the nature of ASD and its implications for learning;

2 understanding the individual child and his particular difficulties;

3 adapting the school environment to enable the child to cope and realise as much of his academic and social potential as possible.

The nature of ASD and its impact on the curriculum

A person with ASD experiences difficulty fully developing a 'theory of mind'. This means that to a lesser or greater extent he will find it difficult to 'mind read'. He will:

- find it hard to understand others' intentions;
- find it difficult to see things from another point of view;
- tend to assume that others know what he knows, so may assume too much knowledge on the part of the listener;
- tend to assume others share his all-absorbing interests;
- not easily understand oblique references, inferences, subtle meanings, non-literal language;
- not share normal teenage interests in relationships, e.g. when teenagers talk together of what he said ... or she meant by ... what happened between x and y in *EastEnders* ...
- find relationships difficult while at the same time having the same emotional needs for security and acceptance as everyone else.

A person with ASD has difficulties in three areas, known as 'the triad of impairment':

a) social interaction

b) social communication

c) social imagination, flexibility of thought and thinking skills

Social interaction difficulties may manifest themselves as

- aloofness;
- social isolation;
- anxiety and distress;
- depression in an older child;
- inappropriate behaviour which becomes worse when the child is stressed;
- difficulties understanding and conforming to group 'rules';
- difficulty understanding social cues in different settings;
- difficulty interpreting non-verbal cues such as body language, facial expressions, tone of voice

Social communication difficulties may manifest themselves in

- poor conversational behaviour, such as
  - interrupting
  - talking too long about his own interests regardless of whether or not this interest is shared
  - keeping to a topic, especially if not of his own choosing
  - answers and comments may appear irrelevant
  - inappropriate volume
  - unusual tone of voice
  - making strange noises
  - echoing words or phrases
  - using over-formal 'grown-up' language
  - obsessive interest in certain topics
  - avoidance of eye contact
- being unable to see another's point of view;
- not realising whole-class instruction applies to him;
- inappropriate understanding of social cues;
- literal understanding;
- poor comprehension of text in contrast to decoding ability.

Social imagination, flexibility of thought and thinking skills – difficulties in these closely related areas may manifest themselves as:

- an inability to imagine what others think;
- an inability to predict others' behaviour and reactions;
- rigid and repetitive behaviour;
- imagining hypothetical situations and outcomes;
- obsessions about favourite videos or books which may be learned by heart;
- stereotyped role play, often with re-enactment of learned situations from favourite videos;
- inflexibility in applying learned behaviours across many contexts whether appropriate or not;
- being upset by changes of routine;
- obsessive behaviour;
- not using language for a variety of thinking purposes such as reasoning, predicting and inferring;
- a limited ability to be creative;
- difficulty generalising knowledge from the situation in which it is learned to another.

Implications for learning for pupils with ASD

- Difficulties co-operating mean they do not learn with and from their peers.
- Difficulties developing conversational turntaking skills may prevent them listening and responding appropriately in discussions, which restricts learning and reduces shared knowledge.
- Pupils with ASD can become distracted by details or their own thoughts and miss the main point, leading to gaps in their knowledge and missed steps in sequences of instruction.
- Too literal an understanding of what is said may impair understanding as well as prevent them from understanding jokes.
- Pupils with ASD often misinterpret the ordinary teasing and banter of other pupils as bullying.
- They may also misinterpret a reprimand as thinking the teacher hates them.
- Reading comprehension tends to be superficial.
- Thinking tends to be inflexible and links between pieces of knowledge are not easily made.
- Limited ability to use their imagination in school often affects creativity.
- Poor thinking skills particularly affect maths, science, history, geography and English because of difficulties reasoning, inferring and predicting.
- The strong desire for sameness and routine means that they respond badly to unprepared changes in timetable, room or personnel.
- Repetitive and obsessive behaviour may show in excessive tidiness, such as being unable to continue writing if there is a mistake (which then has to be rubbed out) or having to start in the same way each time with pens and pencils arranged in a certain way.
- Poor understanding of social cues makes them appear rude, insensitive and offensive. This can make them a target for bullying.
- Inappropriate behaviours – which most commonly arise from the child's attempts to reduce or cut out what he finds disturbing such as noises or emotional demands – can distract, alienate and irritate staff and pupils.
- Social rejection leads to low self-esteem, a sense of failure and depression.
- Anxiety and distress will precipitate antisocial and destructive behaviour.

Understanding the individual child and his particular difficulties

- **All pupils with ASD have special educational needs regardless of their academic ability** and these may be provided for in a variety of ways. Some schools can offer appropriate support through the resources available in school. In other cases the pupil may require additional support over and above what the school can provide (usually through a statement of special educational need).
- Most, but not all, children with ASD have been identified by the end of Key Stage 2. About two-thirds have accompanying conditions, the most common being attention deficit hyperactivity disorder (ADHD) and attention deficit disorder (ADD), dyslexia and dyspraxia. A few children have more than two

of these conditions resulting in additional difficulties such as impulsivity, lack of a sense of danger, attention and listening difficulties, organisational difficulties, reading and spelling problems, fine and gross motor difficulties, fatigue and behaviour difficulties. There may also be medical issues such as epilepsy.

- Many children on the autistic spectrum experience sensory difficulties. This may show as a strong desire not to be touched and/or a strong dislike of certain textures. They are frequently oversensitive to noise and light making negotiating corridors and halls problematic.

- How these difficulties manifest themselves and how much of a problem they are in school seems to relate not just to the severity of the difficulties but also to the mix of individual personality and temperament and how the problems are managed by the family and the school. For the child in school, the school context is the only thing that can be changed.

- The child's history is important in understanding the nature of his difficulties and how best to manage them. Past IEPs should show what has been targeted and what worked (and did not work) to help him achieve those targets.

- Transition between schools, key stages and year groups is most successful when it is planned by people who know the child well and can make sure there is proper liaison. For instance it can be helpful for the child's LSA to take the child to his new school in advance of his cohort, and if possible introduce him to his new LSA or support teacher and/or his mentor. Constructive information can be passed on about his abilities, strengths, difficult areas, strategies and how best to support him. His receiving school and teachers can then be well prepared and staff working with him will have had time to acquaint themselves with his difficulties and the strategies that have worked thus far.

- A pupil profile of the child – with a photo, describing his personality, other children significant to him who may be a support or a negative influence, strengths and weaknesses in subject areas and in school life, trigger points, useful management strategies and current IEPs – is very effective, especially if drawn up by someone who knows the child well. This pupil profile can be given to all teachers likely to encounter the child.

- Giving one person in a school responsibility for pupils with ASD is proving to be very effective. The ASD co-ordinator is the link between staff, child and home, and mediates between them all.

- Liaison with the child's family is also important. Parents and carers know things about their child that others do not. Their observations, concerns and their own management strategies can be helpful as a consistent approach is considered to be the most effective.

Adapting the school environment

This requires a commitment from the whole school and a willingness to adapt to meet the real needs of the child, recognising that a secondary school is a stressful environment for many children, in particular children with ASD.

The ASD co-ordinator

S/he is the person:

- who is the most knowledgeable about the child and who liaises with staff and the child on a day-to-day basis;
- who can provide other members of the teaching staff with advice on room layout, visual schedules, homework policies, rewards and sanctions;
- who is notified by staff of changes that will affect the pupil;
- to whom the child reports every morning so he can be prepared for changes in the school day;
- who distributes pupil profiles and photos of the child to relevant teaching and non-teaching staff including supply teachers, lunchtime supervisors, office and administrative staff, and who makes sure staff know of current issues, behaviour strategies, current IEPs, medical issues and anything relevant to the child;
- who is responsible for liaison with home;
- who organises and arranges staffing for a 'time out' area or safe base within school for the child; he needs to know when and how he is allowed to use the safe base;
- who liaises with the SENCO regarding setting up, monitoring and reviewing of non-curriculum IEPs such as behaviour targets;
- who is aware of possible homework difficulties and can suggest or set up alternative arrangements such as a supervised homework club at lunchtime or after school (open to other children as well);
- who organises break time arrangements appropriate to the child's social difficulties;
- who is aware of the need for staff training and promotes opportunities for staff to liaise with each other regarding the child's progress and response to different classes;
- who is responsible for helping other pupils in school understand something of the nature of the child's difficulties. This requires sensitivity and must involve the parents and the child in saying what they do and don't want others to know about ASD;
- who is able to find out what works in certain situations so that this can be transferred to different, but similar situations;
- who liaises with, or is a mentor for, the child. Times and places need to be set so the child knows when and where he has access to his mentor;
- who tries to anticipate trigger points and problem areas so that confrontation and strain can be reduced or eliminated;
- who makes sure the child has the appropriate support when it is needed;
- who tries to make the child's access to the curriculum as fair as possible;
- who acts as an advocate for the child when he cannot do it for himself.

Teaching staff

They should:

- see a photograph or meet with the child prior to teaching;

- read the pupil profile before teaching the child for the first time so that teaching strategies and differentiation, if necessary, can be prepared;

- know the child's current IEP targets;

- liaise with the ASD co-ordinator and support staff regarding school and class expectations and sanctions;

- make sure the ASD co-ordinator is informed of any changes to the pupil's timetable, staff and room changes;

- create work areas within the class suitable for individual work, supported work, group and class work away from heaters, computers, walkways and other distractions. This may involve setting up some sort of work station;

- be aware of other pupils who can negatively as well as positively influence the child and arrange seating and grouping accordingly;

- consider the most appropriate way to help the child follow a lesson. This may involve simplifying classroom language and possibly reducing the amount of dialogue. It may also mean cutting out redundant comments which may confuse the child;

- make as much learning as possible explicit and unambiguous so the child is not confused;

- be aware that the child may have difficulty understanding non-verbal cues such as facial expression, tone of voice and body language. As a result, his response may seem inappropriate;

- be aware that the child is going to need help to make the necessary links between new and previous knowledge;

- be aware that the child is not likely to see the bigger picture and may become distracted by detail and draw the wrong conclusions;

- help the child respond to extended teacher dialogue by:

- giving a context for listening (as in, 'I am going to tell you about ...', 'This happened over 100 years ago before your grandfathers were born ...')

  - giving a purpose for listening (as in 'This is about how you decide whether the animal is a mammal or not ...', 'This is so you know which order to follow ...')

  - explaining the criteria for success (as in 'By the end you will be able to ...', 'There will be no items left ...')

  - 'chunking' instructions and allowing processing time between chunks

  - giving signposts throughout the instruction (as in 'There are four parts to this activity', 'First of all ...', 'Then ...', 'Next ...', 'After that ...', 'Finally ...')

  - not using idioms without an explanation

- be prepared to differentiate homework imaginatively. Reconsider the necessity and value of the homework in the light of the child's difficulties.

The whole school

- In some cases it is not possible for the pupil with ASD to conform to the school rules because they are not attainable by that child. In these instances, a flexible approach is vital. Expectations and sanctions for that child may have to be modified.

- Make sure the child knows what behaviour is expected of him – he won't understand this unless it is made explicit.

- The child needs to learn his way around school and know how to follow a timetable. He needs to know classroom routines, lunchtime routines, library routines, and so on. He also needs to know what to do when these routines are breached, for instance if he is late for school because of a doctor's appointment or the timetable is disrupted because of a photographer's visit, rehearsals for the school concert or drama production. He needs to learn to whom he should report, where to go and who to ask for help. He needs to know what to do if he is ill or if there is an emergency.

- Homework is often a difficulty and realistic adaptations may need to be made so that the child does not become alienated and can manage to do something useful. It is vital to keep in touch with parents about homework as this can be a huge problem and a major cause of stress at home. A supervised homework club in school may be a possible solution.

- Pupils with ASD are unable to access the curriculum in the same way as other pupils because their condition makes them different, even when they are intellectually bright. They do not perceive the world in the same way as others. In order to give them the best chance to flourish they need understanding, support and differentiation.

An autistic view of the world

Autistic voices

With Donna

This was how I saw things: bit by bit, a string of pieces strung together.

I learned eventually to lose myself in anything I desired – the patterns on the wallpaper or the carpet, the sound of something over and over again ... Even people became no problem. Their words became a mumbling jumble, their voices a pattern of sounds. I could look through them until I wasn't there ...

I could comprehend the actions of another person, particularly if they were extreme, but I had trouble coping with 'whole people' – their motivations and expectations, particularly to do with giving and receiving.

With violence, I knew where I stood. To call it the result of 'baser' emotions must be true, for I certainly found it easier to grasp. Niceness is far more subtle and confusing.

The constant change of most things never gave me any chance to prepare myself for them. Because of this, I found pleasure and comfort in doing the same things over and over again.

The stress of trying to catch up and keep up often became too much, and I found myself trying to slow everything down and take some time out. One of the ways of making things slow down was to blink, or to turn the lights on and off really fast. If you blink really fast, people behaved like in old frame-by-frame movies; like the effect of strobe lights without the control being taken out of your hands.

It was as though, if I concentrated too hard, nothing would really sink in. Unless the task was something which I chose, I would drift off, no matter how hard I tried to be alert. Learning, unless it was something I sought, and taught myself, became closed out and hard to comprehend just like any other intrusion from 'the world'.

Similarly, I would turn the sound up and down on the television, or intermittently block my ears off. This seemed to imitate the difficulty I sometimes had hearing people consistently.

I talked compulsively when I was nervous. I also talked to myself sometimes. One reason for this was that I felt so deaf when I said nothing. It was as though my senses only functioned consistently when I moved within my own world, and that meant closing others out.

(From *Nobody Nowhere: The Remarkable Autobiography of an Autistic Girl* by Donna Williams, Jessica Kingsley Publishers, © 1992 & 1999 Donna Williams.)

With Luke

I had finally found the reason why other people classed me as weird. It was not just because I was clumsy or stupid. My heart lightened instantly and the constant nagging (not my Mum) stopped immediately. I finally knew why I felt different, why I felt as if I was a freak, why I didn't seem to fit in. Even better, it was not my fault! ... I felt like charging out into the streets and shouting, 'Hey, look at me, I have Asperger Syndrome. I am not a freak.'

I can only speak for myself when I say that if one subject is on my mind or I am fascinated by something, then literally everything else is insignificant ... If I am focused on my fascination ... I feel an overwhelming excitement in me that I cannot describe. I just **have** *to talk about it and the irritation at being stopped can easily develop into a raging fury.*

I can spend hours looking at the patterns and shapes around me. I carry in my head my own little show of patterns and prisms and shapes and colours. They intermingle with shapes from the outside world.

When I think of one thing I think of that and only that. When I am spinning or gazing at coloured or flashing things I am oblivious to the world.

I have a strange kind of hearing and can only concentrate on listening to things if I know I am meant to. Distinguishing between background v foreground noise has always been a problem, so however long they shouted I would have presumed it was background noise. This is a difficulty of AS because I get told off so many times for being an ignorant pig when I genuinely do not recognise that I am being spoken to.

When I look someone straight in the eye, particularly someone I am not familiar with, the feeling is so uncomfortable that I cannot really describe it. First of all, I feel as if their eyes are burning me and I feel as if I am looking into the face of an alien ... Sometimes it is hard to concentrate on listening and looking at the same time. People are hard enough to understand as their words are often so very cryptic, but when their faces are moving around, and their eyebrows keep rising and falling and their eyes getting wider then squinting, I cannot fathom all that in one go, so to be honest I don't even try.

There is another thing that I find really annoying and that is the fact that exams are taken in big halls. I can hear everyone turning their pages on the exam sheets and this drives me crazy.

I can't even think about sleeping at night when I have games the next day. I can't concentrate on the lessons before as my worst nightmare is slowly approaching. When it is time for the lesson, I genuinely feel sick and have a headache with worrying. Of course I am told that I will be able to run it off or just ignored completely. It is my worst time at school and I have done all I can to avoid it.

(From *Freaks, Geeks and Asperger Syndrome: A User Guide to Adolescence* by Luke Jackson, Jessica Kingsley Publishers, © 2002 Luke Jackson.)

With Clare

Our concrete learning style seems to be connected to our intense need for routines and predictability. Neurotypical children are able to extract an overall picture of what is going on and safely disregard 'unimportant' details. For us, there is no such thing as an unimportant detail and we may experience great distress if we cannot predict what will happen in our environment or make sense of the changes that do occur.

I could not shift my attention from one subject to another by an act of will; it seemed to take a sort of mental 'wrench' to manage it at all and the level of effort required meant I could only sustain it for short amounts of time before I switched off and was unable to take in any more information.

Often we end up getting 'stuck' and persevering about one detail or preliminary point and unable to get an overview of the project as a whole. Failing to estimate how long a piece of work will take, we may leave it until the night before the deadline, or end up spending all our free time on it because we feel it must be perfect and are unable to tell when it is 'good enough' to count as finished.

'Traditional' forms of teasing and bullying ... are often not classified by teachers as bullying at all, or are treated as jokes, with the victim being treated as a 'bad sport' if they react with humiliation, fear and pain, instead of 'seeing the funny side'.

When teachers did address bullying, they often did so by advising the child with Asperger's on how to act ('act more confidently' 'just ignore them') rather than directly intervening. Putting the onus on the victim to end the bullying in this way is usually ineffective, particularly since children with Asperger's can only obey such instructions in a literal way and typically do not have the social skills to use them flexibly as defences.

Reading about Asperger's is indispensable, but it should be the starting point for teachers working with Asperger's, not the finishing point ... Each child with Asperger's is an individual. Some, if asked, will be able to articulate for themselves what they need in order to learn and how they would like school to be different. Others will not and it will be up to their teachers to listen to the messages conveyed through their behaviour.

... the presence of even one teacher who was willing to approach a student with Asperger's with insight and respect could make a dramatic difference to the whole of their school career and even to their life as a whole (even though that student might not have been able to express their gratitude or provide any positive feedback at the time). Conversely, ignorance and intolerance could scar a child for life.

(From *Martian in the Playground: Understanding the Schoolchild with Asperger's Syndrome* by Clare Sainsbury, Lucky Duck Publishing, © 2000 Clare Sainsbury.)

A comparison of autistic spectrum disorders and neurotypical responses

People with ASD perceive and respond to the world differently from the majority of human beings – the so-called 'neurotypicals' (NTs). They have particular difficulties understanding emotions and socially interacting with others.

Here are some of the ways autistic brains and neurotypical brains seem to differ from each other.

A person with ASD will tend to:	A neurotypical (NT) person will tend to:
see details but not the 'big picture'.	integrate parts to see the overall pattern.
have difficulty understanding the 'rules' of conversation, for example turntaking. His only reasons for stopping would be because he had finished, to take a breath or ask a question.	pick up the rules incidentally, naturally developing awareness of subtle non-verbal cues such as dropping pitch when coming to the end of the contribution, pausing, making eye contact, nodding, so that another can join in appropriately.
be fearful of change and have a strong desire for predictability. Comfort is found through rituals and repetitive behaviour. The need to be in control is shown through the putting of objects in order, inflexibility in responses and through obsessions.	have a desire for new experiences and knowledge and cope with change of routine fairly easily. Their sense of security is likely to come from a secure emotional base and comfort can be found without extreme responses.
find it difficult to acquire higher order comprehension skills which are non-verbal, such as inference, which means that verbal skills may be good but superficial. They may not correlate with other skills, such as self-help skills and social functioning.	find good verbal skills will help to maximise the effect of other abilities and help understanding in other subject areas. They are also more likely to correlate with other abilities and contribute to social functioning.
find it difficult to generalise and be flexible in his thinking. This affects how well he can use what may be good intellectual skills.	find good intellectual skills are more likely to make his education easier.
find multitasking difficult if not impossible. He will tend to perceive through one sense at a time. Information received through two senses, such as talking and showing is likely to be confusing.	can learn to multitask and do some things without thinking.
find it difficult to single out people as separate, unique identities, different from the furniture and other surroundings.	is instinctively aware of people and faces, and can make fine discriminations between people from a very early age.
need to practise social interaction skills in many contexts because of difficulties generalising. He will not learn incidentally from others and will need deliberate teaching.	learn instinctively the rules of interaction through observation and modelling without deliberate teaching. His natural desire to want to belong to a group will assist in learning appropriate behaviours.
experience the outside world as baffling, incomprehensible and terrifying, not helped by his own or others' emotions.	experience the outside world as interesting and stimulating. Emotional support helps overcome fears.
find no value in social approval because there is no innate emotional reward in putting in the effort to behave 'normally' and others' emotions can be frightening.	find it naturally rewarding to be approved of and accepted by others. He will find social approval encouraging and emotional warmth valuable.

A person with ASD will tend to:	A neurotypical (NT) person will tend to:
need help to cope in real situations. Role play is not helpful because the situation is never exactly replicable and is therefore confusing.	find it helpful to be prepared for real life situations through rehearsal and role play.
laugh at inappropriate times. Laughter may arise out of fear or the release of fear or just understanding something. It may be belated because extra time is needed to think things through. He may also have difficulty sharing jokes because this may involve understanding others' viewpoints.	express enjoyment with laughter. It often signifies shared enjoyment and may be 'catching', meaning that a point of view is shared.
'echo' words as a response to stress and the fear of reactions of others. He can step back into the pattern of the sounds and not hear the meaning.	echo words in order to taunt others, having a deliberate emotional intent.
repeat phrases because he knows a response is needed but not what sort. It does mean that there is some sort of relationship expressed because both make the same sounds.	repeat phrases to irritate others. He will usually know what sort of response is required and will not be excessively afraid to be wrong.
hear speech as a pattern of sound. The pattern is the most salient feature so it is easy to lose the meaning and also non-verbal cues such as tone.	respond to the meaning of the words and the tone in which they are delivered. He will tend to ignore features getting in the way of meaning such as accent.
find direct looking and hearing too confrontational, creating too much fear. He will learn better indirectly and will often look away.	find that the more open and direct the look, the more can be observed.
find a fascination for spinning, coloured and shiny objects. This is relaxing because it causes him to lose awareness of himself and distances him from others.	find spinning, coloured and shiny objects interesting but not compulsive, and not serving an emotional purpose.
find that apparently destructive behaviour such as breaking glass as a symbolic separation from others reduces his fears.	express destructive behaviour arising out of curiosity, attention seeking or emotional disturbance.
find that hurting himself or doing something embarrassing will cause a shock to others. This may be because of a desire to control others' reactions, to test how 'real' he is, or to break free of conforming because it is so exhausting and unrewarding.	indulge in these behaviours because of emotional and behavioural difficulties.
avoid physical contact because touch is painful and may only be tolerated as if one is made of wood. Touching hair may be acceptable as it is separate from the body.	welcome physical contact because it is experienced as intimacy and gives comfort and reassurance.
not want others to expect responses from him, such as 'thank you', and prefer things to be put nearby rather than given to him directly.	expect a response as part of the give and take of social interaction and which is mutually pleasurable.

A person with ASD will tend to:	A neurotypical (NT) person will tend to:
would prefer others to speak of him not to him because he does not welcome directness. An indirect approach is interpreted as meaning that the other person is expressing awareness, sensitivity and respect for him.	would think that a lack of direct contact makes someone appear indifferent, cold and shifty.
only accept physical touch if nothing is expected and it is free and casual, otherwise all touch must be initiated by him, or at least for him to be given a choice.	experience lack of touch as neglect, rejection or coldness.
need a lot of courage to speak out, so it is important that he is listened to and respected for his effort, but not directly.	value responses of others and find recognition gratifying.
have a strong desire for privacy and space. His sense of isolation comes from inside and is not connected with being left to his own devices.	feel isolated and without structure if left on his own for too long.
find it most difficult to cope with others' emotions. His greatest fears are the expression of love, kindness, affection and sympathy, and living up to others' expectations. He most values informed understanding, a detached manner and indirect responses.	thrives on receiving and expressing love, kindness, affection and sympathy and is socialised by expectations. The lack of the expression of these emotions would appear as indifference and lead to dangerous emotional isolation.

Resources

Behaviour

All Year Round: Exciting Ideas for Peaceful Playtimes, Jenny Mosley and Georgia Thorp, LDA (also available from www.winslowpress.com).

Anger Management: A Practical Guide, Adrian Faupel *et al.*, David Fulton Publishers (www.fultonpublishers.co.uk).

Autism – PDD, Creative Ideas During the School Years, Janice Adams, Adams Publications (available from www.winslowpress.com).

Broken Toy, Tom Brown, Lucky Duck Publishing (www.luckyduck.co.uk).

Challenging Behaviour and Autism, National Autistic Society (www.nas.org.uk).

Crying for Help: The No Blame Approach to Bullying, George Robinson and Barbara Maines, Lucky Duck Publishing (www.luckyduck.co.uk).

Making a Difference, Sharon Lissaman and Elaine Riley, Northumberland County Council and Cleveland County Council.

Names Will Never Hurt Me, Tom Brown, Lucky Duck Publishing (www.luckyduck.co.uk).

Nurturing Emotional Literacy, Peter Sharp, Smallwood (www.smallwood.co.uk).

Thinking and learning

Brill the Brave, Mike Lake, Questions Publishing (www.education-quest.co.uk).

Listening Skills: Early Years, KS1, KS2, Sandi Rickerby and Sue Lambert, Questions Publishing (www.education-quest.co.uk).

Look, Listen and Think, Jean Edwards, Prim-Ed Publishing (www.prim-ed.com).

Looking and Thinking Books 1–4, Arthur J. Evans, Learning Materials Ltd (www.learning.materials.btinternet.co.uk).

Mapwise: Accelerated Learning through Visible Thinking, Oliver Caviglioli and Ian Harris, Network Educational Press (www.networkpress.co.uk).

Primary Thinking Skills, Mike Lake and Marjorie Needham, Questions Publishing (www.education-quest.co.uk).

Reading & Thinking Books 1–3, Arthur J. Evans, Learning Materials Ltd (www.learning.materials.btinternet.co.uk).

Teaching Children with Autism to Mindread, Patricia Howlin *et al.*, Wiley (www.wiley.com).

Think About It Books 1 & 2, Learning Materials Ltd. (www.learning.materials.btinternet.co.uk).

Think It Say It, L. Martin, Communication Skill Builders.
Top Ten Thinking Tactics, Mike Lake and Marjorie Needham, Questions Publishing (www.education-quest.co.uk).

Conversation skills

Comic Strip Conversations, Carol Gray, Winslow Press (www.winslowpress.com).
Functional Language in the Classroom, Maggie Johnson, Clinical Communication Materials, Manchester Metropolitan University, Elizabeth Gaskell Site, Hathersage Road, Manchester M13 0JA.
Emotions/Facial Expressions, 9 cards and instruction sheet, Black Sheep Press (www.blacksheeppress.co.uk)
It Takes Two to Talk: A Parent's Guide to helping Children to Communicate, Ayala Manolson, Hanen Centre (www.specialneeds.com).
Talkabout, Alex Kelly, Winslow Press (www.winslowpress.com).

Sensory and motor

Dancing in the Rain, Annabel Stehli, Doubleday, Georgiana Institute (www.georgianainstitute.org).
Developmental Dyspraxia: A Practical Manual for Parents and Professionals, Madeleine Portwood, Durham County Council, David Fulton Publishers (www.fultonpublishers.co.uk).
Dyspraxia: A Guide for Teachers and Parents, Kate Ripley *et al.*, David Fulton Publishers (www.fultonpublishers.co.uk).
Hands On: How to Use Brain Gym in the Classroom, Isabel Cohen and Marcelle Goldsmith, Edu-Kinesthetics (www.braingym.org.uk).
Sensory Integration and the Child, A. Jean Ayres, Western Psychological Services (available from amazon.com).
Smart Moves, Carla Hannaford, Edu-Kinesthetics (www.braingym.org).
The Sound of a Miracle, Annabel Stehli, Doubleday, Georgiana Institute (www.georgianainstitute.org).

Language and communication

Circle Time, T. Bliss and J. Tetley, Lucky Duck Publishing (www.luckyduck.co.uk).
Developing Circle Time, T. Bliss *et al.*, Lucky Duck Publishing (www.luckyduck.co.uk).
Personal and Social Education for Primary Schools through Circle Time Activities, NASEN (www.nasen.org.uk).
Quality Circle Time, J. Mosley, Lucky Duck Publishing (www.luckyduck.co.uk).
Social Use of Language Programme, Wendy Rinaldi, NFER-Nelson (www.nfer-nelson.co.uk).
Spoken Language Difficulties: Practical Strategies and Activities for Teachers and Other Professionals, Lynn Stuart *et al.*, David Fulton Publishers (www.fultonpublishers.co.uk).

Social skills

All the Games Kids Like, Diane Schoenfield Barad, Communication Skills Builder.
The Friendship Factor: Helping Our Children Navigate Their Social World – and Why it Makes for Their Success, Dr Kenneth Rubin (www.thegraycenter.org).
Social Stories, Carol Gray, Winslow Press (www.winslowpress.com).
Socially Speaking, A. Schroeder, LDA (www.ldalearning.com).
Young Friends, S. Roffey *et al.*, Cassell (www.cassell.co.uk).

General

Accessing the Curriculum for Pupils with Autistic Spectrum Disorders, Gary Mesibov and Marie Howley, David Fulton Publishers (www.fultonpublishers.co.uk).
Asperger Syndrome: Practical Strategies for the Classroom, Leicester City Council, National Autistic Society (www.nas.org.uk).
Asperger Syndrome: A Practical Guide for Teachers, Val Cumine *et al.*, David Fulton Publishers (www.fultonpublishers.co.uk).
Asperger's Syndrome: A Guide for Parents and Professionals, Tony Attwood, Jessica Kingsley Publishers (www.jkp.com).
Autism in the Early Years, Val Cumine *et al.*, David Fulton Publishers (www.fultonpublishers.co.uk).
Autistic Spectrum Disorders: An Introductory Handbook for Practitioners, Rita Jordan, David Fulton Publishers (www.fultonpublishers.co.uk).
Jenison Autism Journal. Quarterly magazine on various aspects of autism covering topics such as bullying, homework, siblings, friendship, bereavement, telling children about their diagnosis, etc. UK distributor: c/o Keith Lovett 199/201 Blandford Avenue, Kettering, Northants UK NN16 9AT.
Supporting Children with Autism in Mainstream Schools, Diana Seach *et al.*, Questions Publishing (www.education-quest.co.uk).

An autistic view of the world

Autism: An Inside-Out Approach, Donna Williams. Jessica Kingsley Publishers (www.jkp.com).
The Curious Incident of the Dog in the Night-Time, Mark Haddon, Jonathan Cape (www.randomhouse.co.uk).
Freaks, Geeks and Asperger Syndrome: A User Guide to Adolescence, Luke Jackson, Jessica Kingsley Publishers (www.jkp.com).
John – 'A Big Boy of Nine': A Parent's View of Asperger Syndrome, Lynda Bannister, Lancashire Research Project for Autism.
Martian in the Playground: Understanding the Schoolchild with Asperger's Syndrome, Clare Sainsbury, Lucky Duck Publishing (www.luckyduck.co.uk).
Nobody Nowhere, Donna Williams, Jessica Kingsley Publishers (www.jkp.com).
Somebody Somewhere, Donna Williams, Jessica Kingsley Publishers (www.jkp.com).
Standing Down Falling Up: Asperger's Syndrome from the Inside Out, Nita Jackson, Lucky Duck Publishing (www.luckyduck.co.uk).

Thinking in Pictures, Temple Grandin, Vintage Books (www.randomhouse.com).
Understanding and Working with the Spectrum of Autism: An Insider's View, Wendy Lawson, Jessica Kingsley Publishers (www.jkp.com).

Websites

www.nas.org.uk National Autistic Society. Provides information about publications, schools, training, helpline and information service.

www.oaasis.co.uk Office for Advice Assistance Support and Information on Special Needs. Provides free information sheets, chargeable publications, conferences and seminars, helpline and details of the Hesley Group residential schools.

www.thegraycenter.org Carol Gray's website for publications and the journal *Jenison Autism Journal* (formerly the *Morning News*). This is a newsletter edited by Carol Gray for young people with autism, published quarterly. Includes a section for pen pals. Also useful for parents and teachers. Details from roslord@email.com.

www.tonyattwood.com For helpful advice and papers, resources and books covering Asperger syndrome and social skills.

www.autism.org For information about autism for parents and professionals.

Games

www.incentiveplus.co.uk For games and activities including the Anger Solution Game and Feeling Fair Game.

www.luckyduck.co.uk. For games and activities to address bullying and promote social and emotional wellbeing.

www.smallwood.co.uk Many games and activities available to help develop conversation, social skills, expressing emotions, friendships, teamwork, including Face your Feelings Book and Cards.

National courses

Jenny Mosley INSET Courses For positive behaviour in school and lunchtimes, self-esteem, anti-bullying, teambuilding and circle time. Tel: 01225 767157, www.circle-time.co.uk.

NAS Training and Consultancy, Nottingham. Tel: 0115 9113362, www.oneworld.org/autism_uk

Ros Flack/Phil Roberts ASSET (Autism-Specific Support, Education & Training) Contact Ros or Phil on 01598 710692 for autism-specific courses and in-house training.

Sinet, the Sensory Integration Network provides national courses and special interest groups. 26 Leopardstown Grove, Blackrock, Co. Dublin, Ireland.

Index of areas of difficulty

Helping Children with Autism to Learn

Stuart Powell

This book considers how autistic children can be enabled to learn through specific approaches to teaching that draw together understandings of how they think, and the implications for those who aim to teach them.

£18.00 • 128 Pb pages • 1-85346-637-9 • 2000

Autism in the Early Years

A Practical Guide

Val Cumine, Julia Leach and Gill Stevenson

Anyone meeting a young child with autism for the first time will find this book invaluable. The authors provide extensive material that will be equally accessible and relevant to anxious parents, teachers and professionals who are working together in an unfamiliar area.

£18.00 • 112 Pb pages • 1-85346-599-2 • 2000

Autism and ICT

A Guide for Teachers and Parents

Colin Hardy, Jan Ogden, Julie Newman and Sally Cooper

'This workbook has much to offer... [The authors'] enthusiasm and creativity entice the reader to try ICT and they offer many practical suggestions.'

Computers and Education

£16.00 • 112 Pb pages • 1-85346-824-X • 2002

Accessing the Curriculum for Pupils with Autistic Spectrum Disorders

Using the TEACCH Programme to Help Inclusion

Gary Mesibov and Marie Howley

£17.00 • 144 Pb pages
1-85346-795-2 • 2003

The Autistic Continuum:

An Assessment and Intervention Schedule

Maureen Aarons and Tessa Gittens

nferNelson
understanding potential

The Autistic Continuum enables you to gather insightful information relevant to the understanding of children aged between 2 and 8 years with a spectrum of autistic or autistic-like difficulties. It helps you to decide what to look at, how to interpret the information and how to use it appropriately.

It provides practical and useful guidance on administration, expanding on the items contained within the Schedule and includes a helpful account of the wider implications of specific behaviours.

Manual Incorporating Schedule • 4615 01 4 • £72.90

The Gilliam Autism Rating Scale

James E Gilliam

nferNelson
understanding potential

The *Gilliam Autism Rating Scale* is a rapid behavioural checklist that helps to identify and diagnose autism in individuals aged between 3 and 22 years. Standard scores and percentiles are provided and a table is given for determining the likelihood that the individual is autistic.

This resource is quick and easy to administer and provides comprehensive information regarding the severity of the disorder.

The Complete Set contains an Examiner's Manual and 25 Summary Response Forms.

Complete Set • 4016 00 4 • £110
Summary Response forms • 4016 01 4 • £40.75

From

nferNelson
understanding potential

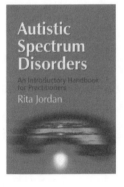